DRIVING BACKWARDS
ON A ONE-WAY STREET

Praise for
DRIVING BACKWARDS ON A ONE-WAY STREET

Laverne H. Bardy's middle initial must stand for Hilarious, which is what her new book is. In *Driving Backwards on a One-Way Street* the laughs come from all directions. I like Laverne and surely you will, too.

—Jerry Zezima
Nationally syndicated humorist
www.Jerryzezimablogspot.com

Any time I need to kick back, forget my troubles and giggle, I read Laverne H. Bardy. She strings words together so well that they could put a smile on a corpse. Her secret is to give her readers a snapshot into her wacky world while making good use of her own funny bone to make it through herself. Reading Bardy is how I and so many others make it through.

—Cappy Hall Rearick
Nationally Syndicated Humor columnist
Author of 16 books including the Glad Girls Mystery series

I love Laverne H. Bardy's sense of humor. It's rich. It's sassy. And her stories create colorful, sometimes embarrassing scenes that I relate to. She has her finger on the pulse of humanity. Whether it's a story about an industrial strength spandex bathing suit or one about strange creatures swimming in her toilet after a power outage, she'll surprise you on each page.

—Akaisha Kaderli
Syndicated columnist
Co-Author, *Your Simple Path to FIRE*
RetireEarlyLifestyle.com

Those who laughed out loud while reading Laverne H. Bardy's first book, *How the (Bleep) Did I Get This Old?* will get the chance to laugh out loud again and again with her latest, *Driving Backwards on a One-Way Street*. She nails all ages with a bawdy, funhouse mirrored reality that comes in all sizes and shapes.

—Rita Robinson
Award-winning former newspaper reporter
Author of eleven books

Memoir essays that touch the heart and tickle the funny bone. *Driving Backwards on a One-Way Street* is a portable mood lifter.

—Lorraine Ash
Author of *Self and Soul*

One of the funniest writers around, Laverne H. Bardy will be better for your mood than a visit to the Botox doctor.

—Sheila Moss
HumorColumnistBlog.com

DRIVING BACKWARDS ON A ONE-WAY STREET

A SAVVY SENIOR'S MAP TO FINDING HUMOR IN EVERYTHING

LAVERNE H. BARDY
SYNDICATED HUMOR COLUMNIST

Driving Backwards on a One-Way Street
A Savvy Senior's Map to Finding Humor in Everything

Copyright @ 2020 Laverne H. Bardy

ISBN 978-0-578-66302-9

Laverne H. Bardy
lavernehb@gmail.com
www.lavernebardy.com

Cover illustration by Marc Cicchetto
Graphic design by Bill Ash

Cataloging-in-publication data

Driving Backwards on a One-Way Street

p. cm.
ISBN 978-0-578-66302-9
PCN

1. Humor—Observational 2. Memoir—Bardy 3.Humor—Women
4. Newspaper—Columns—Syndicated

PS3552 B059 2019   814.54 BA

200407

CONTENTS

Contents

ACKNOWLEDGMENTS

Hugs to my loving husband, Marc Cicchetto, whose support was boundless and who patiently adjusted to fend-for-yourself dinners and my daily technology rants.

Heartfelt appreciation to Lorraine Ash, my editor and memoir writing workshop coach, for guiding me through long periods of indecision and confusion while graciously sharing her time, wealth of knowledge, and generous heart.

INTRODUCTION

D RIVING BACKWARDS ON A ONE-WAY STREET is a collection of seventy-one of my nationally syndicated humor columns. Each column showcases humor extracted from my life; guaranteed to lift your spirits, bring a smile to your face and, in many cases, cause you to laugh out loud.

The book includes stories about my struggle to get out of and back into a soaking wet, one-piece, industrial-strength bathing suit; and how a 50-plus friend had her breasts super-sized and became an exotic dancer. It's about how I dealt with my husband's retirement (not well), my battle with a box of almond cookies, how my electric scooter betrayed me, and my appalling experience with an uncooperative suppository. It's about a stranger who motivated me to continue walking when painful arthritis was fighting to keep me from reaching Macy's cosmetic department.

People often express their belief that I am fortunate to lead such an interesting life. Actually, my day-to-day life is quite conventional. What may be different is the outcome of my obsession with eavesdropping, and poking my unsolicited nose into people's business. What I overhear while in a diner or waiting in line at the market, is no different from what most people hear. The distinction is, I suspect, that I enjoy taking time to not just listen, but to interact.

Despite what my parents taught me, I talk to strangers—a lot. I'm not too shy to ask strangers to please elaborate or clarify what I just overheard them say while I was listening in on their conversation. I've been doing that for years and have never been faced with a negative response. I approach people with a non-threatening smile, and they are usually happy to talk about themselves. I am a curious individual who enjoys writing about those observations and experiences—often with exaggeration.

While my everyday life is not unique, my perception of it may be. I believe that developing the ability to see past the obvious is the key to a fascinating, fun-filled life. You needn't do more than open your eyes and ears, and be mindful of how easy it is to transform ordinary into extraordinary, and mundane into memorable.

DRIVING BACKWARDS ON A ONE-WAY STREET

THE FAIRER SEX

LET IT ALL HANG OUT

My friend Sue was in her mid-fifties when she decided to be an exotic dancer. I did my best to talk her out of it, but she had friends who danced—all younger than she. They were making great money so she thought she could, too. Her goal was to work until she saved enough to open a specialty bakery. Then she would quit.

Sue had an excellent body for a woman her age. She was raking in upwards of $250 a night, but she wasn't content. Other dancers, most of whom were named Barbie, made double that amount. Sue was convinced it was because the Barbies were better endowed. In the business of selling fantasies to men, size definitely mattered. Men's tips grew in direct proportion to the size of the breasts they ogled. Whether they were the real deal or surgically enhanced made no difference.

Sue took her bakery shop savings and made an appointment to have her girls enlarged. To assure that she would pull in big bucks, she said, "Heck, I might as well make this surgery worth it. Let's supersize these cupcakes, Doc. How about building me a set of 46DDs?"

Until then I never knew a woman could hold up that kind of weight without falling to her knees.

We made plans to meet for lunch a few weeks later. I was already seated when Sue's enhanced appendages rounded the corner and entered the room a full minute before the rest of her. When I finally saw her face, she was beaming.

"Well? What do you think?" she asked, flaunting them in my face. "And if you think they look great now, you should see them when I lie down. They stand right up, perky as all get-out, which does make sleeping on my stomach somewhat challenging, but you'll never hear me complain. I'm pulling in close to $500 a night."

"There's something unnatural about that, don't you think?" I asked. "When I lie on my back and watch TV from bed, my girls accommodate me by flattening like deflated tires. By the way, since your feet always travel in the shadow of those mountains, don't they get cold?"

A month later Sue and I took a vacation to France. The resort we stayed at had a topless beach. Not one to be mistaken for bashful, Sue ripped off her bikini top and set those babies free. Within seconds half the men on the beach were focused on her 46DDs.

"What the hell are they staring at?" Sue grizzled.

"You didn't expect to unleash those puppies and have them go unnoticed, did you?"

"All I know is when they were smaller men never paid this kind of attention to me. Now, suddenly they're interested."

"You are kidding, right? Isn't this what you wanted? Could it be they're staring now because you didn't look like this before? Or maybe it's all innocent and they're taking bets on whether you can walk without tipping over onto your nose."

"Not funny."

Times certainly have changed. When I married the first time, I was barely twenty-one years old, with a shapely figure. On our honeymoon I wore a demure, fitted, red wool dress with a sweetheart neckline that revealed less than one-half inch of cleavage. The first gift my husband ever bought me was from the little shop in the Catskill resort where we stayed. It was a small heart-shaped gold and pearl brooch intended to cover my barely existent cleavage. Apparently, he was afraid someone might mistake me for a woman.

Little did I know that would be the most romantic gift he would ever give me. For our first anniversary he gave me a toaster.

Today's moral standards are the antithesis of those pounded into my head in the 1940s. I was taught what good girls did and didn't do. Back then having a good reputation was critical because it would arrive at any given place before I did. People would judge me by it.

I'm not thrilled with the huge swing the pendulum has taken in the sexual revolution. What I am is conflicted. Sometimes I think about how much fun it might have been to wear a scanty bikini back when I had a great figure to flaunt, instead of those industrial-strength one-piece suits carefully designed to reveal little more than neck and knees.

I hope I'm around when the pendulum finally comes to rest.

HOW THE HOME SHOPPING NETWORK TURNED ME INTO A ZEBRA

was channel surfing and landed on the Home Shopping Network. I had assumed that people who buy from HSN were either housebound, lonely, or certifiable. Why would anyone purchase items they can't first touch, smell, taste, or try on?

Two women, each with perfect hair, chicklet smiles, and saccharin voices, were promoting stretch jeans. They waved their hands, à la Vanna White, and described the color, texture, pockets, stitching, and thrill of being able to remove them at the end of the day and not find a red ring around their waist. Red ring? How was it I'd never had one of those? I felt cheated.

I never knew so much detail could be ascribed to a pair of pants, other than they come with a waistband, zipper, and two openings for legs, which I don't recall them mentioning at all.

Callers phoned in, swooned, and agreed that since they'd been wearing those jeans, they, too, didn't have red waistband rings. It became my mission to find someone with a red waistband ring and make them show me what I'd been missing.

Celia, from Atlanta, called and admitted to already having seven pairs of "those incredible jeans." She decided to make it a nice round number by ordering five more.

"They're absolutely wonderful," she oozed. "I wear them for just about everything: digging in the garden, working at the

9

office and, with the right accessories, I've even worn them to weddings and bar mitzvahs."

As they listened to Celia's review, the two saleswomen, barely able to contain their excitement, salivated. They reminded viewers to not wait another moment.

"Get to your phones or computers and order immediately. We've been advised that there are only eight hundred sixty-three pairs of these unique jeans remaining, and you do not want to miss out on this stupendous offer."

I was prepared to switch channels when those two honey-tongued sweeties brought out a product that clutched at my heart: Tan Towels. Self-tanning towelettes.

I live in New Jersey. I hadn't seen or felt sun on my body in more than five months. I looked like I'd been dredged in flour. A few hours earlier I remarked to my husband that it was time to head south. I had begun to blend in with the walls.

The camera zoomed in on a model's arms. One was pasty white, like mine. The other was a golden tan. She slid a moist Tan Towel over her untanned arm. We viewers were assured that within minutes she would look like she just returned from two weeks in Hawaii.

Before I could think it through, I reached for my credit card and phoned the number on the screen. I knew I had to do it immediately because there were only 6,057 Tan Towels left, and the phone lines were lighting up.

I made the fateful call and returned to the television, afraid I might miss something. Margaret was extolling the magical wonders of Tan Towels, which she had purchased at an earlier date.

"I've been using them for several months now," she said. "They make me look and feel so good."

Sugar dripped from her lips as one of the beauties asked, "Margaret, would you mind telling our audience your age?"

"Not at all," she said. "I'm eighty-four, and my boyfriend says I've never looked better."

The saleswomen could hardly catch their breath.

"Did you hear that?" one of them gasped. "Margaret is eighty-four and still cares how she looks. How absolutely adorable."

I froze in my tracks. Was there a cutoff date for caring how I look? I was seventy-four. Margaret was eighty-four, which meant, if I was really lucky, I might have ten years of caring ahead of me. I made a note to go to Google and find out exactly how long it would be before I no longer gave a damn.

My Tan Towels arrived. I couldn't wait to start smearing them over my body. The HSN ladies assured me that my color would never turn orange or streak.

I hadn't realized that since Tan Towels go on clear, there was no way to know whether I was overlapping areas. Also, I couldn't reach my back.

I now look like a member of the animal kingdom with leathery brown knees and elbows and a zebra-striped body. Somehow, I managed to totally miss my hairline so I look like I'm wearing a white headband.

The whole purpose of buying these things was to give me a head start on my tan. We're leaving for Florida in a week. There's no way I can be seen looking like this.

Does anyone know where I can buy a lightweight, summery burka?

I AM WOMAN

Recently I got hooked on the TV show, *What Not to Wear*. Apparently, the show has been around for a number of years but somehow had eluded me. It features two fashion gurus, Clinton and Stacy.

Every week they select one clueless, style-challenged woman whose entire wardrobe consists of sweats, yoga pants, hoodies, pajama bottoms, and lettered T-shirts. They offer her a five-thousand-dollar gift card to buy all new clothes if she's willing to hand over her current wardrobe. If she agrees they subject her to humiliating put-downs as they rifle through her wardrobe and question the pathetic thinking that prompted her to buy each and every item. This is done under the guise of enlightening her.

I am not fashion conscious. I can honestly say that I've never spent a cent on Vogue, Allure, Cosmopolitan, or any fashion magazine, for that matter. If you ask me the brand name of the blouse or slacks I'm wearing, I would have no idea. I buy whatever appeals to me and looks good on me. I'm more into style than fashion. The difference, as I understand it, is that fashion is short-lived and style, with a few accessory updates, is ageless, which is why you're likely to see me wearing the same clothes year in and year out—with new earrings.

Watching this show, I learned that all eighteen of my beloved turtleneck shirts are passé, and older women in particular shouldn't wear them because they accentuate jowls. I gave a moment's thought to their expertise but quickly decided that displaying my jowls was far less offensive than highlighting my wattle.

The most confusing thing I learned from this show is that clothes do not have to match. Rather, they have "to go." Neither Clinton nor Stacy explained what that meant, but Clinton made that statement while wearing a black V-necked pullover sweater with a large red diamond design in the center, over a pale blue and white checkered shirt. The colors and pattern combinations ignited my gag reflex faster than Ipecac syrup. But his kelly-green loafers were the pièce de résistance that had me racing to the porcelain throne.

The positive side of not having to match clothes is that my wardrobe selection has grown exponentially. No need to spend time coordinating outfits. Just jump into a pair of maroon slacks and pull on an orange sweater. It's a tremendous time-saver and wonderfully freeing.

I am one of seven women in the nation who actually dislikes shopping. Because arthritis makes walking difficult, nearly all of my shopping is done online. But I do periodically buy a few garments when seasons change. Empowered by my new education, I drove to the mall where I knew I'd have the widest selection.

I tossed my walker into the trunk, drove a half hour to the mall, removed the walker, and began my trek. I tried on about thirty outfits and selected five I was convinced would meet with Clinton and Stacy's approval. When my back, hips, and legs rebelled, I knew it was time to leave Macy's and head home. But I still needed a specific lipstick, only available in malls.

When I was told the cosmetic department was on the opposite side of the store, I stopped walking and heard myself say aloud, "That's not going to happen. My pain is too intense."

I was about to turn and retreat when a woman, maybe in her late seventies, came up from behind and grabbed my upper arm.

"We are women," she said with authority. "We don't allow pain to stop us from doing what we want. Get to that cosmetic department. Now! I have a bad toe that makes walking extremely painful, but I'll be damned if that's going to stop me from getting to the jewelry department."

Then she was gone. Like the Lone Ranger.

I swear, I felt as though I'd been injected with a vial of high-octane fuel. I focused on getting to Cosmetics, and my pain took a back seat.

That stranger will never know how her words impacted me that day, and most days, since. Each time I think I can't go another step, I feel her firm grip on my arm and hear her empowering words: "We are women! We don't allow pain to stop us."

IT'S NOT FAIR

I was born a 100 percent female. Don't get me wrong, I love being a woman. And by no means am I scatterbrained or helpless. But would it have hurt if I'd been given a small dose of testosterone? Just enough to allow me to understand something about how my car works. Just enough so that when I hear a flapping noise under the hood, I'd instinctively suspect I have a bad belt and don't need a new transmission, like the mechanic insists I do. The fact I'm on the far side of fifty doesn't help. Mechanics seem to believe that wrinkles replace brain cells.

I want the confidence of knowing that if I change my own flat tire, it won't fall off while I'm cruising the turnpike.

I have a girlfriend who may have received my share of testosterone at birth. Macho Maggie not only loves cars but knows each by its name, year, and model. The only vehicles I readily recognize are 18-wheelers, yellow school buses, and old model Volkswagens. All the rest look alike.

With rare exception, I can't stomach sports, either. My ex was a sports fanatic. Nothing else interested him. After twenty-three years with him I developed a Teflon attitude toward sports in general and baseball in particular. Words such as "home base," "shortstop," and "fly ball" no longer compute. They slide right off my brain.

Football has been explained to me more times than I care to recall, and still I don't understand why the opposing team refuses to let the guy carrying the football run the length of the field the way he wants to. If this one rule were changed, the game wouldn't have to drag on so long.

I want to be able to distinguish fullbacks from tight ends. Actually, I'm pretty good at recognizing tight ends, but only off the football field.

At Super Sunday parties I want to care when a team has only one down to go. I want to understand how four minutes left in the game really means forty-five minutes. I want to be more interested in the game and less in the chili dogs being passed around, and I want to drink beer without gagging.

I want to derive an erotic sensation from gliding my hand over a drill press in a mega-hardware store and experience joy while watching shoot-'em-up movies.

I'd like to slouch in a chair with my legs uncrossed and relaxed and not give a thought to what may or may not be a "ladylike" posture.

I want to roll down my car window while I'm driving, spit with conviction, and not have it blow back into my face.

If there's a way I can learn to do all these things and still maintain my integrity as a feminine female, I want to know. As things are now, it's just not fair.

MY CUP RUNNETH OVER

A n observant friend noticed that I appear to have become, shall we say, "bustier" over recent years. She was right. My bra size had noticeably increased in direct proportion to my age. But it had nothing to do with mammary, and everything to do with memory.

It started when Age began her insidious journey through my body. Over the years I became aware of little "gifts" she bestowed upon me—a strand of gray here, a wrinkle there, here an ache, there an ache, everywhere an ache, ache. (Sorry, I just spent the weekend babysitting my grandchildren.) Body parts that had been perfectly content with their home for years packed up and moved south.

Okay, I'm a modern woman. I can get my hairdresser to do something for my gray and a competent plastic surgeon to help me fight gravity, but my greatest problem involved my most precious asset—memory. I was rapidly running out of it.

Attempts to improve or compensate for my fading memory failed until one day, as I wandered the aisles of an office supply store trying desperately to remember why I was there, I spotted a selection of colorful sticky notes. It was then I decided that carrying sticky notes with me at all times would allow me to write down my thoughts the moment they occurred. I wouldn't have to rely on my memory. But where could I put them to ensure that I'd find and read them?

The answer came as I watched an old movie and observed Cary Grant give Mae West a piece of paper with an address on it. She folded it in half and slipped it into the top of her gown's scoop neckline. At that moment I realized my bra was the one constant in my life—and an excellent depository for notes.

As my years advanced, and my memory further diminished, I stuffed more and more notes into my bra. As a result, my A cup grew to a C and then a D. Well, one side did. My right-handedness had me listing to the left, so I had to retrain myself to stuff messages with my left hand as well.

The best part of this process is the excitement I experience when I disrobe each evening and watch scores of messages flutter to the floor. When I scoop them up and read them, each is a complete surprise.

My only concern, as I get older, is what will become of me. I can see future headlines now:

Police were summoned to the home of 90-year-old Laverne H. Bardy, found lying face-down on the floor of her bedroom today, kicking and thrashing wildly in a futile attempt to stand. Bardy, whose upper body weight refused to budge, was heard mumbling something about an urgent need to visit an office supply store. Her children were notified. After assisting authorities in hoisting her to an upright position, they managed to sedate her with a fresh package of pastel sticky notes.

Somebody, help me, please, before this scenario becomes reality.

MAKE UP YOUR MIND

I received a cold call.

"I'd like to speak with whomever handles the finances," a male voice said.

"That would be me."

Pause.

"May I speak with your husband?"

"Which is it?" I asked. "The person who handles the finances, or my husband, because my husband can barely add?"

Longer pause.

"Okay, then I'll talk to you."

"I'm sorry," I said. "I don't do business with chauvinists."

And I hung up.

That felt good. But it would have felt better if I'd had an old phone that allowed me to slam down the receiver.

MY LiFE AS A PiONEER

Hurricane Irene struck in August, leaving us powerless for four days. We have an all-electric house, which meant no refrigeration, lights, water, air conditioning, or flushing ability. But temperatures weren't at their usual scorching highs, so it was bearable. Mighty Marc filled toilet tanks with water from our pool, and we boiled bottled water for pasta, canned soups, and tea on our outdoor grill. Food spoilage was minimal because my resourceful husband repeatedly shoved store-bought ice bags into refrigerators and freezers. We frantically shopped for a generator, but the smart people had already bought them.

On the fifth day power returned. By the sixth day thoughts of generators had flown from our heads.

The last week of October another quirk of nature struck in the form of a snowstorm. I awoke at 1:25 a.m. for one of my treks to the bathroom and smashed into the corner of my dresser. Ouch! The night-light that always guides my way was not lit. Nor was my digital clock. Oh no. Not again!

I woke up Mighty Marc. Something had to be done to keep our small Caique parrot warm. We took Molly from her overindulgent three-by-five-foot cage, relocated her to a small cage in front of our propane fireplace, and covered it with two large beach towels. Molly is not used to having her cage covered so we anticipated some reaction in the morning.

We determined not to open our refrigerators or freezers throughout the outage, no matter how inconvenient. Then we piled on extra blankets and went back to bed.

In the early morning I was awakened by a string of desperate hellos from Molly's cage. The poor bird had no idea where she was. We kept her in front of the fireplace while we phoned the pet shop where we board her when we vacation. They had power and said they'd take Molly.

A foot and a half of snow had blanketed northwest New Jersey, so Mighty Marc dressed in winter wools, dragged out his plow, and carved a path from the garage, up our steep driveway, to the street.

Pumpkins on our front deck turned to mush. Mums on our lawn keeled over and snapped under the weight of snow. The left half of our beautiful, once perfectly symmetrical Magnolia tree dropped to the ground. Two cherry trees uprooted and fell over. One landed on our deck. Another half dozen trees lost many huge branches. It was sad. We love our stately trees.

Our country road was closed to through traffic on both ends. Trees had fallen on power lines. To exit our street we had to circumvent dangling branches and wires. We held our breath and crossed our fingers each time we bypassed orange cones and raced through.

Life in the dark was not so romantic this time. We were freezing. Our fireplace helped, but not much. Our pool was closed, but our neighbor's wasn't, so Mighty Marc lugged pails of green murky water up a hill to fill our toilet tanks. On one occasion I was preparing to sit when I spotted a floating, dead pollywog. Also, a lively black insect was skating across the water. One of those had bitten me in my pool. No way was I going to lower my behind. Mighty Marc came to my rescue, armed with a pasta strainer.

We drove around a lot, often aimlessly, saw two movies, and ate out twice a day.

As nighttime crept in, we rounded up solar lights from our patio, bunched them into bouquets, and placed them in vases. Wearing layers of clothing, we played board games in the light of five small flashlights dangling from our dining room chandelier. Candles in our shower stall served as a night light.

Personal hygiene was nonexistent. I considered showering at my gym, but I hadn't been there in four months, so I didn't have the courage to show up with a bar of soap and a towel. My hair no longer needed hair spray to stick in place, so I made an appointment with my hairdresser, just to have it washed.

To our amazement, when we opened our freezers, after four-and-a-half days, everything was frozen solid.

Our first order of duty was to buy a generator.

I learned that I would never have survived as a pioneer. Without hot water, a curling iron, and a microwave, there's no valid reason to get out of bed.

VANITY

BATTLE OF THE BULGE

I was swimming at a Cancún resort when I exited the pool for a bathroom break. In the stall I removed my cover-up and looked for a place to hang it. There was no hook. The stall door was so high, I couldn't sling my coverup over it. So I folded it and held it between my teeth.

I ripped off several strips of toilet paper and placed them on the seat the way my mother had taught me, because everyone knows that toilet paper is the prophylactic most doctors recommend to prevent venereal diseases.

My bathing suit was one piece, crafted to conceal rather than reveal, which pretty much guaranteed that men's eyes would avert, not flirt, and ignore, not explore. It was the style worn by matronly, plump women who would be only too happy to pierce one of their own eyes with a fishhook if doing so meant they would once again fit nicely into a bikini.

I stuck my thumbs under my soaking wet steel-belted straps, forced them down over my shoulders, and jimmied my elbows out from under. I wondered why God, in His infinite wisdom, had opted to create boneless breasts. Other than to nurse infants and titillate men, they are useless. Boneless breasts are good only in chicken recipes. I have to stuff them into tight, strangulating bras, and when I lie on my stomach on the beach, I'm forced to scoop out individual holes for them, or they flatten, spread out, and come to rest in my throat, which makes breathing challenging. If my breasts had bones they could have assisted in my struggle to pull them out of my suit. Instead, they just hung there, pretending they weren't involved, and did nothing more than get in the way of the cover-up still dangling from my teeth.

I took a deep breath and continued to push the suit down to where it refused to go. I shoved and wiggled, but it remained passive.

Time had become an issue.

Several more gigantic shoves and it slid to the floor, just in the nick of time.

But my toughest challenges lay ahead.

I bent over and grabbed hold of the sopping wet coil hugging my ankles, but the wad of fabric in my mouth made it impossible to see what I was doing. A solid five minutes of backbreaking tugging got the suit back up to my hips, but no further.

I was trapped in a Mexican toilet and held hostage by a floral print boa constructor.

I wondered if my husband had noticed how long I'd been gone. I thought about shouting, but I wasn't about to let anyone rescue me in that condition.

It was then I saw the pipes on the wall in back of the toilet. I removed the cover-up from my teeth, tucked it between the pipes, and kept battling with my bathing suit.

Several lifetimes later I succeeded in getting the suit all the way up, no thanks to my two useless girls. I reached for my cover-up, and the unthinkable happened. It slipped from my fingers and dropped into the toilet. What to do? Who was I kidding? That cover-up could have been a diamond-encrusted Diane von Fürstenberg original, but there was no way in hell I was going after it.

I exited the restroom and walked toward my lounge chair. As I prepared to sit, a woman several chairs away beckoned to me.

"Excuse me," she smiled. "I don't want to embarrass you but there's a long strip of toilet tissue stuck to your back and another one behind your right thigh."

Saying "thank you" didn't seem appropriate, so I giggled, nodded, and reached for the wet paper on my back. When it only came off in tiny strips, I asked my husband to help. As he peeled off the paper, he said, "I understand how it may have attached itself to the back of your thigh, but I'm curious to hear how it got stuck to your back and shoulders."

I picked up my sunglasses, hat, and book, and dropped into my lounge chair.

"It's not something I care to discuss. Maybe someday, but not today."

COOKiE MONSTER

Y esterday I did something I hadn't done in years. I pigged out. I stuffed a whole box of cookies down my throat, in record time.

"Why?" you ask.

If you do not understand pigging out, then nothing I say here will interest you. Either your eating habits are under control or you actually prefer carrots over carrot cake. In any case, we can't possibly relate, so you're dismissed.

While I do suffer from periodic bouts of Overeateritis, pigging out is not usually my style. Stuffing chocolate bars in my glove compartment, under the driver's manual, for later consumption, is more my style.

After dropping Mighty Marc at the doctor for a routine visit, I browsed through a nearby Trader Joe's market. If you've never shopped at a Trader Joe's, be grateful. I never leave that store without depleting my checking account. It sells healthful, gluten-free, and organic foods. Unfortunately, none of those adjectives rule out the extensive variety of calorie-laden goodies they also carry. Had I the brains of a peanut, I'd have shopped next door for shoes instead.

My shopping cart was overflowing with multigrain breads, high-fiber spelt crackers, raw almonds, brown rice, and organic vegetables, when I spotted the cookie display. I swear those cookie boxes blinked and beckoned me with flashing neon letters.

I don't even like store-bought cookies, unless you count Mallomars and chocolate-covered graham crackers, which I allow to enter my mouth once a year after swimsuit season has passed and I know the inevitable collateral damage can be camouflaged with bulky winter sweaters.

The description on the boxes said "thin, crisp, almond cookies." I tried to ignore them, but no matter what I did they winked and screamed passionately like high-spirited Gospel singers:

We know you can hear us.
We know you're not blind.
Please let us contribute
to your ample behind.
Say Hallelujah!

I wanted to stay on course and not give in to impulse buying, but those damn cookies wouldn't let up. People were staring, which forced me to return to the cookie aisle, yank a box off the shelf, and slap it into my shopping cart. Anything to make them shut up.

Even before I reached the car, my trembling hands tore open the box. One taste and I was hooked. I sat them beside me in the car. As long as I shoved those scrumptious monsters into my mouth, they were quiet. The minute I stopped chewing they started screaming, so I pulled over, jumped out of the car, and stuffed those loud-mouthed demons into the trunk.

I picked up Mighty Marc from the doctor, drove home, and placed what was left of the cookies on my kitchen counter. Realizing I was in danger of polishing off the entire box, I handed the nearly empty box to my husband and asked him to please hide them from me. He winked and asked, "What's my reward?"

"A slim wife," I answered as I grabbed the cookies back from him.

Tossing the cookies into the garbage wasn't an option. I've been known to retrieve chocolate from the trash and scarf it down before you could say "bacteria."

In less than fifteen minutes I devoured the entire box of cookies and promised myself I would get back to dieting Monday—a yarn I'd been known to spin nearly every Sunday of my life. My stomach gurgled, undulated, and swayed with each step I took.

As retribution for my sin I forced myself to go to the gym on a day I wasn't scheduled to be there. I lifted weights, did sit-ups, and rode ten miles on the stationary bike. I'm proud to say I worked off twenty-seven of the 3,496 calories I consumed.

Overeating is an enormous problem in the United States. Apparently, it even extends to wildlife in my part of rural New Jersey. Driving to the gym, I saw a sign that read, "Heavy Deer Area." I have to wonder what this world is coming to when overweight deer are segregated from slim ones.

WEiGHTY SiTUATioNS

'm allergic to many foods. Soon after eating them I break out in fat. My husband can eat anything he wants and not gain an ounce. I deeply resent him for that. I don't think he ever heard the word "calorie" before meeting me. But his lack of knowledge in this area often works to my advantage. He'll watch me wolf down a bucket of Breyer's. Two days later, when I cry, "I don't understand. I do everything right and still I gain weight," he sympathizes and explains that everyone's metabolism is different and I shouldn't be so hard on myself.

When I started Weight Watchers for the twenty-first time I told everyone I knew that this time I would lose the weight. This time, I said, I was confident and highly motivated. Then, one morning I opened the fridge, reached for my usual cottage cheese and blueberries, and discovered something was wrong. Something was missing—my motivation. It was nowhere to be found.

Shortly thereafter, I ran into a friend who asked how I was doing on my diet.

"I lost ten pounds in ten days and kept it off an entire ten minutes," I said. "Sorry you missed it."

There have been several times in my life when revealing my weight was essential. Once I was with two friends boarding a plane so small that passengers were asked to submit their weight to the flight attendant. We stopped in our tracks and looked like we'd just been caught in the closet with Ben and

Jerry. We didn't know what to do: tell the humiliating truth, or lie and be responsible for killing a plane full of people.

We agreed to let everyone die.

Once the plane took off we realized that we'd be included in the death toll. We beckoned the flight attendant and confessed. To our surprise, we were told they automatically tack on fifty pounds to whatever number women give them. We were offended that they assumed women would lie.

A few years later, when my arthritis became increasingly worse, Might Marc and I ordered a chairlift to take me up the stairs from the garage level to the first floor. Chairlifts come with different weight-carrying limitations. I wanted one that could safely hold the maximum weight, allowing for any future pounds I might gain. Mighty Marc told me I was crazy.

"Even if you carry several bags of groceries on your lap, it'll never come to three hundred fifty pounds," he said.

"But what if I load up on canned goods, a five-pound bag of sugar, and ten pounds of potatoes, all at the same time?" I pleaded. "I'd feel compelled to toss one potato at a time up the stairs, rather than chance carrying them all at once. And, what if—?"

"It's not gonna happen," he insisted.

I gave in. He's probably right, but I live in fear of becoming a humiliating headline:

WOMAN GAMBLES WITH DEATH IN VAIN AT-TEMPT TO CONCEAL WEIGHT FROM HUSBAND.

In a bizarre accident yesterday, Laverne H. Bardy was found spread-eagled on her basement floor after tumbling and crashing from a chairlift that was unable to carry both her and her groceries up one flight of stairs. As paramedics removed potatoes from her face, her husband questioned how this could possibly happen since the chair was built to carry two hundred fifty pounds and his wife only weighs one hundred twenty.

Bardy had no comment.

MY IMPERFECT BODY

I watched the Academy Awards. I swear those people never age. I was in awe of all the beautiful faces and bodies. Well, maybe they do age, but, after all, how tacky would it be to show up in a new $40,000 designer gown, wearing yesterday's face and breasts?

I was especially alert to the fact that nobody jiggled or bounced, until one of the pre-show interviewers revealed that virtually everyone's body was harnessed and held in place by Spanx and other body shapers. Everyone's body, that is, but Jennifer Lopez's. Her perky breasts appeared to have minds of their own, with no intention of being upstaged by the lovely gown attempting to fence them in. They refused to be covered, confined, or overlooked, as they fought to break loose from textile restraints.

My husband and I took bets on which one would break loose and win the race for freedom. We agreed that if she had stayed on stage a few minutes longer, the left one would have won. It had already begun to show signs of upstaging the right one. We were happy to have TiVo because when Lopez and her girls left the stage, we realized we never noticed the actress who presented with her. We went back to see.

Anyone who wants to look as good as possible wears Spanx. For those living under a mushroom, Spanx are thin, tight-fitting underpants—a second skin that pulls you in and smooths out all traces of unwanted flesh and flab. They come in various styles and lengths and can make you look ten pounds slimmer.

I bought my first pair after seeing the shock and revulsion on the face of a size-six exhibitionist in the public dressing room at Loehmann's. She pirouetted in front of a three-way mirror, wearing a red string bikini, when she caught sight of my fully packed body.

"Ya' know," she said in a Valley Girl way that had every statement sounding like a question, "you don't have to look like that?"

"Like what?" I asked, trying hard to pretend I wasn't aware of her insulting implication.

"Like that?" She pointed to my semi-naked, scarred, been-around-the-block-a-few-times, rippled torso.

"You can wear Spanx and look much slimmer," she said, "and none of those lumps will show?"

I looked down at my stomach, remembering I'd last seen my feet in the fall of 1981.

"I used to have a body just like yours," I said. "It never occurred to me that it would change. But this is the result of four pregnancies, twenty-three surgeries, eighty years of living, and an intense hatred of the gym. Watch out, or this could be your future, Sweetie. See it and weep."

Apparently, I am the only living person unable to wear Spanx. I purchased three pairs, in various styles and sizes, and I don't know how to get into any of them. I'm far slimmer than some of the hugely overweight people I know who are comfortable wearing them. Some wear Spanx every day, even under jeans. I don't understand how they get into them and walk. And breathe, too.

I'm learning to appreciate my imperfect shape. As I was lying in bed watching the Academy Awards, I realized I felt sorry for all the women with breast implants. Most are unable to see the television screen when they lie in bed. I, on the other hand, have no problem at all. When I lie on my back, my girls rest comfortably in my armpits; just as God intended.

I'M HAViNG A PHYSiCAL FiTNESS FiT

I hate exercise! Nothing about sweating, exhaustion, and pain appeals to me. The most active thing I did this week was struggle to rip open a bag of Fritos.

Every day the media reminds me I'm out of sync with the rest of the world. The government is presently designing a dollar bill on which running shoes replace George Washington's face. Sweat was officially added to the list of American symbols, along with apple pie, the flag, and Mom. Ellen DeGeneres is promoting a line of bridal warm-up suits, and deodorants are being phased out and replaced with cans of Instant Sweat Aerosols.

Last week I hosted a support group for a group of men and women who shared a common bond—their utter disdain for exercise. One by one, they entered my house, lethargic, sluggish, and overweight. There was a time they accepted who they were, but the world's obsession with physical fitness had interfered with their lifestyle and left them feeling disgraced and embarrassed.

The first despondent person spoke.

"Hello, my name is Portia Portly and I am a non-athlete."

She was greeted warmly.

"I couldn't bear the stares any longer," she sobbed. "Everyone could see I was overweight and out of shape, so I bought a tennis outfit to wear in the supermarket and various other public venues. It's not at all flattering but snarky jeers have been replaced with encouraging cheers."

Portia's idea was applauded and adopted as future policy.

"I joined a health club," confessed a substantially pudgy businessman. "When I tell my macho associates, they're impressed. They needn't know I only go there for massages and smoothies."

I felt compelled to cleanse my conscience.

"When my husband returned home from completing his sixth marathon, he found me lying in the yard. How could I admit that while he'd been running more than twenty-six miles, I'd been sunbathing? So I lied and told him I'd sprained my ankle doing jumping jacks and was waiting for him to carry me indoors."

Everyone empathized.

"A perfect example of prejudice toward non-athletes happened to my cousin, Martha," announced a woman who preferred to remain nameless. "Martha devised an affordable way to extract energy and create affordable fuel from fifty-year-old diet pills she'd found in her medicine cabinet. She received presidential praise and was even up for a Nobel Prize when the bomb dropped. An in-depth interview with Martha revealed she was not committed to being physically active. As a result, her credibility became suspect and she is currently under close surveillance by both the CIA and Richard Simmons."

The meeting concluded after twenty minutes, when the food ran out.

If you feel out of place because you don't smell from perspiration, don't need a knee brace or cortisone shots, and don't own a terry cloth headband and fluorescent running shoes, join us next Saturday at 10 a.m. in front of the YMCA. Be prepared to march for your right to be a sloth because sluggish people matter.

Please be prompt as the parade is scheduled to last only ten minutes. The local first aid squad will be on hand for those who require treatment for exhaustion.

WARM FUZZIES

HE'S RETIRED

H e's retired.

He says that it would make sense to move dishes to a lower shelf, so I don't have to reach so high to get them. And that pantry items would be easier to find if they were in alphabetical order. Also, if I wash clothes with cold water, I won't have to separate darks, colors, and whites.

I growl.

I like my dishes up high. I sit on my ass at the computer, most of the day. The only exercise I get is reaching for dishes and repeatedly picking up my cane from the floor. I tell him alphabetizing pantry items is a good idea and, when he's done, he should tape the list onto the pantry door. And I'm pretty sure cold water doesn't sanitize.

He's retired.

What he loves most is going out for breakfast. Every morning. It was a treat the first 253 times but after eating eggs scrambled, eggs poached, eggs over easy, and eggs fried every day, I'm overdosing. Oatmeal makes me gag. Pancakes make me fat. I suggest we eat dinner out every evening instead.

He's retired.

Holy #$@%, he's a morning person. I don't remember him ever being a morning person. At least not in a way that affected me. It seems mornings are when his creativity, energy, and libido are strongest. It's when he most enjoys talking, especially about his dreams. Whoever said dreams only last a few seconds forgot to tell him. His unabridged versions last longer than most movies.

Mornings are when he enjoys everything noisy—practicing his flute, practicing his violin, listening to classical music and television. Not watching it. Just listening to it as he wanders from project to project. Whistling.

I don't do mornings. I do everything I can to bypass mornings. Generally, I struggle to lift my head from the pillow after a sleepless night during which I staggered to the bathroom at least three times. Mornings are when I need peace, quiet and, in a perfect world, solitude. I don't talk and I'm not remotely interested in listening. It's the time of day when I ruminate, marinate, contemplate, and speculate. My head is full of fresh ideas I can't wait to write about, but I'm tired and lethargic, and my arthritic back and neck hurt. If and when I'm able to focus, I need silence. Without interruptions. Do not talk to me. Do not play the television and do not even think about acting on your libido.

He's retired.

Now that he's home all day, he likes to snack. Just a little. Not much. Just something to tide him over before dinner. Like lunch. I don't do lunch. Not for me. Not for him. I prepare one meal a day. Dinner. Sometimes. He opens the refrigerator and asks, "Where's the milk?" I point. He expected to find it behind the lemon juice, where it was yesterday. I remind him the refrigerator isn't alphabetized, and sometimes we have to move things to see other things.

He's retired.

I'm working at my desk. I hear his footsteps coming down the hall. They're getting closer. He knows I'm working. He enters the room anyway, bends over, and plants an impromptu kiss on the back of my neck. Not something I'm accustomed to in the middle of the day. He sets a cup of hot tea on my desk.

It's flavored exactly the way I like—lots of lemon. He hands me a bracelet I'd asked him to repair. A stone had fallen out. He fixed it. Also, he says our washing machine no longer dances across the floor. That's fixed, too. So is the latch on the front screen door. He asks if I'd like to take a break—drive into town and hit Dairy Queen. I grin. Broadly.

He's retired.

He has no one to play with. Yet. Until he finds a golf buddy and a weekly poker game, I guess I'm it, which isn't entirely bad. Maybe tomorrow we'll take another break. One that involves his creativity, energy, and libido.

WHiLE HE'S WAiTiNG

I sleep with a sticky note pad alongside my bed. Before turning off the light, I write down a project I would love to work on next: a huge collage, decorative birdhouses, quilting, guitar lessons, or an idea for another column or book. Then I turn off the light and go to sleep. Writing down my intention temporarily deletes the thought from my mind and allows me to fall asleep without worrying I'll forget about it by morning.

I also jot down thoughts that cross my mind in the dark, during the middle of the night. When I awaken and read them, it's not uncommon for me to scratch my head and ask, "What the hell does this mean?"

Recently, as I prepared for bed, I came upon a sticky note that had fallen under my end table. It was a reminder to start working on a specific project. I'd written the note several days earlier. Though thoughts of the impending project had been exciting just days earlier, I had completely forgotten about it.

Some people are great achievers. They have numerous interests and can always be found working on one stimulating project or another. I would kill to be one of those people. I've had serious memory problems all my life, and aging exacerbates the condition. I make plans in the evening and forget them by morning. I attend celebratory affairs. Several weeks later I don't remember having been there. And I've never been able to memorize anything. I once prepared a speech for Toastmasters. On a three-by-five-inch card I wrote the keyword, "father," because I had planned to relate a humorous incident about my father. I stood at the podium and stared blankly at the card. I had no idea what the word "father" was supposed to trigger.

I even sought help from a doctor who suspected my problem is either chemical or electrical. He surmised that my synapses don't connect. It is my opinion that they actually repel each other the way like ends of magnets do.

My husband, Mighty Marc, has countless interests he looks forward to working on every day. The difference between us is that he thinks about what he wants to do in the evening and still remembers it in the morning. And when he's engrossed in a project, he can't be distracted. In an effort to get his attention, I once walked up to him and shoved my face directly into his. He swatted like it was an annoying mosquito and continued working. I have tap-danced, juggled knives, and offered sexual favors. Nothing distracts him.

I envy his ability to not get sidetracked. He has an internal shade that automatically lowers to block out the world. What I have is a Venetian blind with broken slats that allow everything in. I am distracted by buzzing flies in the next room, leaves swaying outside my office window, chirping birds, air currents, and the whirlpool of thoughts searching for a resting place in my brain.

He is repeatedly praised for his talent and accomplishments. Yes, he is amazingly creative and versatile, but what the world doesn't realize is that he completes each of his projects because of me.

We're retired, so most mornings we enjoy going out for breakfast. All he has to do is pull on a shirt and a pair of jeans and he's ready to leave the house. I require more time and work, so he usually attends to one of his projects while he waits.

A phrase such as "I'll be ready in a minute" gives him ample time to create a full chapter of the book he is writing.

"I still have to feed the cats" allows him time to carve out a neck for the violin he's making.

"I only have to apply lipstick" has him pounding out the first movement of the classical score he's composing.

"I just need to put on earrings" affords him plenty of time to build a frame for his latest oil painting.

As you can see, I am a necessary part of his creative process. Okay, I'm not exactly his muse, but bottom line is, it's because of me that he's able to achieve so much.

Do I get credit for any of this? Never. To be honest, I'm angry my role in his successes has never been recognized or viewed as significant. But, if I run true to form, by tomorrow I will not remember that I am irritated. We will plan to go to breakfast, and while I decide which shoes to wear he will probably scale Mt. Everest.

PUPPY LOVE

I was closing down my computer for the night and, as always, first checked my messages. To my surprise, I found a string of forty-seven Facebook messages I'd never seen. Dates ranged from early 2013 to early 2015. Since I check my messages every day, and it was then mid-2016, I was baffled. Where had these messages been hiding for three years? And what prompted them to show up now, all together? Even stranger was the fact I knew none of the senders.

There were a handful from unscrupulous scoundrels from foreign countries, claiming their parents/husbands/children had died and left them destitute. They each knew, just from looking at my picture, that I had a kind heart and would be more than happy to deposit a million dollars into their accounts so they would no longer have to be homeless and endure incurable diseases. They also knew that they would, one day, visit me in America and we would get married, and they would get their green cards. (Okay, they never mentioned green cards.)

One message was from a man named Tom. He'd read a blog post I'd written titled "Don't Count Me Out," about an elderly woman who held up traffic as she struggled to push her walker across the street. He had loved the piece and thanked me profusely.

I felt terrible. Three years had passed and I hadn't responded to his eloquent, thoughtful words. I answered him immediately.

But the most exciting message was from a man whose name I suddenly recognized. He had sent it three years earlier: "Did you spend two weeks at Coney Island during the summer of '47? If so, then I was the little boy up the street who had a mad crush on you. Marty Radner"

My skin tingled. Marty Radner!

We met when I was nine and he was eleven—an older man. He had spotted me on the beach and told his buddy he wanted to meet me. He made that happen the following day when we met "by accident" on the sidewalk near the cottages our families were renting. He asked how long I would be there. I said we were going home the next day. He asked for my address so he could write, but I don't think he ever did. That had happened just shy of seven decades earlier.

I had been as taken with him as he had been with me, but other than that brief encounter, we never met or spoke again.

Over the years I thought of him often. I'd never experienced such feelings. I couldn't clearly remember how he looked, but I understood that what we felt back then, at such tender ages, had been inscribed on our hearts.

"Puppy love" is defined as an intense but relatively shallow romantic attachment typically associated with adolescence. I suppose that's what it was, but that experience taught me to never dismiss a young person who claims to be in love. What they feel is real and strong. And if it's a first-time feeling, it will be there to call upon for the rest of their lives.

My heart raced as I searched for Marty's Facebook page, saw his picture, and read the abbreviated version of what he'd been doing all these many years. Our lives had followed similar, creative paths.

I wrote: "I sure hope you aren't a hoax. I've been in trouble several times for trusting people on Facebook, only to find they were sleazy. That said, I just came across a note you wrote to me three years ago, asking if I was the little girl, back in 1947, who spent time in Coney Island. I AM THAT GIRL!! In fact about a year ago I was searching Facebook for you, but there were so many Marty Radners, I gave up. This is so weird! I had a mad crush on you, too. We were in Coney Island for two weeks. If it's you, feel free to contact me. Laverne"

He did.

We have since exchanged numerous Facebook messages, but seventy years is a lot to catch up on. I learned that when he spotted me on the beach back then, he thought I looked like Esther Williams, which caused me to laugh out loud—a nine-year-old Esther Williams. Amazingly, he remembered I was from Union, New Jersey and had lived on Erhardt Street, but neither of us remembered whether he had written.

We are both happily married and live a considerable distance from each other, so we may never meet. But it has been a lovely experience going back in history and recalling a warm and wonderful feeling.

GooD INTENTioNS

After it snowed all night, our street looked like a magical fairyland. But all that beauty translated to more than a foot of white stuff on our long, steep driveway.

I had peeked out the window on my way to the bathroom at 5:15 a.m., feeling happy it was Sunday and I had no commitments. I could remain in bed until 9:00 when our parrot would demand attention and food. I'm pretty sure she swallowed an alarm clock during one of her demanding rants because she knows to start screaming at exactly the same time every morning.

I got back into bed and pulled the quilt over my head. I'd barely fallen back to sleep when I had to get up and feed our outdoor cats. They have heated floor pads in their individual little cat houses as well as heated food and water dishes. Usually I find them standing with their noses pressed against our French door, waiting to be fed. That morning was no exception. Their fur was fluffed up and thick to help ward off the cold. For years I concerned myself with thoughts of how horrible their lives must be during the winter cold, but I've come to understand they don't seem to notice or mind it. I've seen them sitting on our deck railing, sunning themselves in 15-degree weather.

Mighty Marc would be getting up any minute. We have an indoor/outdoor thermometer in our hallway. When I left food for our outdoor cats, I noticed it read 2 degrees Fahrenheit outdoors and 68 indoors. I lit the fireplace and scurried back to my comfy bed.

My digital clock flashed 7:32. I dearly wanted to get some more sleep. I repositioned myself under my warm quilt when my husband got up and dressed. Within minutes I heard the loud whirl of our snowblower, powered by Mighty Marc. I peeked out the window and saw him bundled up in a heavy, camouflage-pattern jacket and pants, boots, a fur hat that covered his ears, and a white mask that kept cold air from entering his lungs.

I was grateful for his stamina and incredible attitude. I love the fact that he never complains about the tedious chores that fall onto his shoulders. In fact, he never complains about anything he has to do. He accepts everything life hands him with a smile—from changing a lightbulb, to taking out trash, to plowing a foot of snow. To him, they're all jobs to be started and finished without whining.

I'm nothing like him.

I crawled back to bed with loving thoughts of what nice thing I could do for him. Since breakfast is his favorite meal, I decided to surprise him with a lovely one: waffles with warm syrup, eggs over easy, crisp, dry bacon, and hot chocolate with whipped cream.

Eventually, I fell back to sleep but, as predicted, our parrot, Molly, yelped, making it clear she was officially awake and wanted to be acknowledged. Mighty Marc usually takes care of her. They share a special love. I do not feel warm fuzzies for Molly, although she is a beautiful bird. Her flight wings are clipped because, left to her own devices, she would eat every piece of wooden furniture in the house, but not until she first pooped on everything. More often than not, her demands interfere with my thoughts, my serenity. But since Marc was outside, I fed her, then carried her to a perch in front of the window where she could watch the love of her life pushing snow around. She called out to him to no avail. He heard nothing over the roar of the machine he pushed.

I was tired of all the interruptions and anxious to grab a few more minutes in bed.

The next thing I knew, Mighty Marc was leaning over and giving me kisses from his warm heart and his ice cold nose. I smiled and said, "You've worked so hard. How would you like a special breakfast?"

"I'd love it," he said. "That's exactly what I was thinking. Get dressed. We're going out to breakfast."

I'm no dummy. I was up, dressed, and out of there in twenty minutes flat. Why would I bother to make him the same thing he could order at our local diner, where we could leave the dirty dishes behind?

My mother used to say that the road to hell is paved with good intentions. I should arrive there any minute.

HONEY-DO

G rowing up in the 1940s, I learned that a wife's role was to be pleasant, accommodating, and unassertive, and husbands were to have the final word in, pretty much, everything. If my parents had disagreements, they were careful not to let us know. Since I had never seen conflict between them, I had no idea how to deal with it in my marriage. When my first husband and I had our first disagreement about dust he spotted on top of the refrigerator (I hadn't realized I was supposed to clean areas I couldn't see), I thought that meant we were headed for divorce. Consequently, I did everything possible to maintain peace.

This wasn't always easy, especially when something needed repair. He had no interest and even less aptitude when it came to things involving nails, ladders, and hammers. Rather than phone a repairman, though, he'd procrastinate and vow to fix it himself (sometime before he died).

For the most part, I put up with it. Until my electric garage door broke. It was then I was forced to reach deep within and find my inner grit. I refused to get out of the car and open the door under my own power in bad weather.

Over the months I repeatedly asked him to either fix it himself or call someone who could. I begged, threatened deadlines, whined, and explained what a tremendous inconvenience it was. His response was always the same: "I'm going to do it" and "I said I'll do it."

There is no doubt that had it been his garage door, it would have been repaired promptly. Today I question why I never pulled my car into his side of the garage and claimed it as mine.

It would have been great to have a husband who enjoyed tinkering with tools, a man who took pride in how his home looked and enjoyed pleasing his wife.

l left the marriage after twenty-three years and savored every moment of being single for the next twenty-three. I am fiercely independent and planned to never remarry. There was no longer a need to hold back my feelings, to yield to someone else's desires, or to compromise.

Floral carpeting? Why not? Company for dinner? Naaa. A restaurant instead? Definitely. Vacation in Italy? Sounds great. I loved the freedom and spontaneity that came with living alone. And I had phone numbers for several reliable repairmen.

When I wasn't looking, along came Mighty Marc—the antithesis of my ex-husband, a man I'm pretty sure was born with a toolbox in his hand. I liked his face. I liked his smile. I enjoyed his humor and loved his attentiveness, but his skill with tools is what had my heart flip-flopping and saying "yes" to his marriage proposal.

And now, all I have to do is think out loud, "Hmmm, I wonder how that lamp would look on the other side of the room," and before I take another breath, he's up, running, and moving the lamp. He's so fast, I often feel the need to begin every sentence with, "It doesn't have to be done now" because if I don't, it will be done before I've completed my thought.

My voice activates him.

A short while ago our home was renovated. Mighty Marc did 90 percent of the work himself. The job was complete except for hanging photos and artwork. I didn't need him for that. I'd hung scores of items on walls. It's simple. I eyeball the area where I want the painting to go, hammer a nail into the wall, and hang the artwork on it. Period.

Time? Under a minute.

I made the mistake of saying, "I think tomorrow I'll finally get to hanging the paintings and photos."

It was as though I'd shot a starter gun. He was instantly off and running to the basement. He returned with wire, picture hooks, a T square, drill, calculator, string, blue chalk, staple gun, tape measure, step stool, and compass. Okay, not a compass, but that's because he couldn't find it.

I watched him work out the calculations, and stood back in awe, grateful I hadn't attempted the job myself. I had no idea that the effortless way I'd been doing it my entire life was wrong, and that picture hanging was intended to be complicated and time consuming.

This must be why my parents never argued. My mother learned early on to sit back with folded arms, smile, and allow my father to create mountains out of molehills, so he could feel needed and appreciated.

YOUNG AT HEART

We were seated outdoors at a romantic seaside restaurant in Puerto Vallarta. A waiter walked over and asked for our drink order.

I looked up at him and had to catch my breath. He was about twenty-eight, with jet black hair, deeply tanned skin, pearly white teeth, and a killer smile that showcased two perfect dimples. He was flawless.

He smiled, took our drink order, and headed for the bar.

I leaned into Mighty Marc and, in a thick, husky voice I found hard to conceal, I said, "Oh ... my ... God, that boy is breathtakingly gorgeous."

"Would you like to take him home with you?" he laughed.

"Well, if you wouldn't mind. Maybe just for a few hours."

When the waiter returned Marc said, "My wife thinks you're very handsome, and would like to take you home with her."

Then he turned back to me and flashed a devilish grin. I wanted to disappear. I wished I were wearing sharp, pointy-toed high heels so I could kick my beloved husband in the shin hard enough to leave a dent.

Instead, I smiled.

"Yes," I said. "I would like to take you home with me. My husband said I can, if you'll agree to it."

We all laughed. The tension was broken.

At the end of the meal I had to go to the restroom. It was then I remembered my walker, which was several feet away, against a wall. Normally my arthritis has me using only a cane, but because we planned to do a lot of walking and shopping, I'd brought my walker, which offers more support. Instantly I regretted that decision.

I looked across the room where Mr. Magnificent was leaning against the bar speaking with another server. I didn't want him to see me pushing a walker. I'd been flirting like a schoolgirl. He had responded with playful winks and smiles. And now, I was about to confirm what he already knew, but I had pretended he didn't: I was old and needed a walker.

Suddenly, my timeworn body reminded me of what I would never be again. Young. Pretty. Desirable.

I adore my husband. He never lets a day pass without expressing his love for me and his belief that I am beautiful. That has always sustained me. Just not at that moment.

I wondered if I could make it to the restroom without using my walker. I took several steps and realized I probably could, but without it, I moved with the grace of a zombie.

The object of my affection saw me hobbling toward my walker, which was roughly a table's length away, and came running to my rescue. He grabbed the walker and rolled it to me. As if that wasn't humiliating enough, he proceeded to lead me to the restroom where he pushed open the door and ushered me in, all with the panache of Vanna White gesturing toward the winning contestant's brand new car.

As the door shut behind me, I was painfully in touch with the cruel reality that flirting and walkers go together about as well as hot pastrami on white bread with butter.

Several weeks later Mighty Marc and I were sitting in a diner eating breakfast. It was a Sunday and the church crowd had all converged at the same time. On line waiting to be seated was an elderly woman, maybe in her mid-eighties, leaning heavily on her walker. She and her husband were laughing. It was apparent the woman had a crackerjack personality when, with both hands gripping her walker, she did a kind of dance, gyrating her hips in a humorously suggestive manner, then kicking one foot up at a time like a Radio City Rockette. She had a radiant smile and contagious laugh. The small crowd encircling her was captivated. She was someone I would have liked to know. Neither her age nor her disability mattered. She was delightfully playful, young at heart, confident, and at peace with who she was.

This woman had granted me an aha moment. I suddenly realized that a person's true self shines through whether she is standing on her own or leaning on a piece of metal, and that youthfulness is a state of mind, not a state of body.

I'd like to believe Mr. Magnificent saw me in the same positive way that I viewed this fun-loving, high-spirited woman, who just happened to be old.

MY HUSBAND THE OPTIMIST

We'd planned on going to the gym and coming directly home because I had a great deal to do. But after the gym we realized we hadn't eaten, so we stopped at the diner for breakfast.

Then I remembered I still hadn't picked up a replacement clock for the bedroom. Our other clock had melted when I set it on my electric Salton cup warmer that I'd inadvertently turned on, resulting in a gooey, plastic puddle of clock. So we went to Bed Bath & Beyond.

Along the way I mentioned that I felt guilty flitting around when I had so much desk work and writing to do. Then I remembered a jewelry advertisement I'd read in the paper and remarked that I'd like to go to that jewelry store one day the following week.

Marc got excited and said, "Let's go now."

I reminded him that I really shouldn't. I'd mapped the day out the night before and so far, other than the gym, I'd not done anything I'd planned. He laughed, made a U-turn, and headed east.

"Forget your plan," he said. "Learn to be flexible. This will be fun."

I had a terrific time selecting baubles at the jewelry store but, operating in my usual worrywart mode, I thought that if we left immediately we could get home in time for me to squeeze in several hours of work.

Marc suggested that since we were in the area, we could go for sushi at our favorite Japanese restaurant. How could I resist? I love sushi, so I agreed and thoroughly enjoyed the food. But my grumbling and worrying continued.

It was then Marc said, "You have to learn to live in the moment. You know you will always find time to do those things you need to. We've just shared a beautiful, spontaneous day. It was wonderful. Life is wonderful. Learn to relax and enjoy it."

The next morning he informed me that he was going food shopping without me, so I could stay home and do my work. It was a Saturday, a day when supermarkets are generally mobbed. But that Saturday promised to be even worse because a blizzard was predicted for that night, and people were stocking up.

When Marc came home, laden with heavy bags, I jokingly asked, "Did you have a good time?" To my amazement he answered, "Yeah, it was fun."

"Fun? Fun? What part of fighting crowds and waiting in lines was fun?" I asked.

"I don't know," he shrugged. "It was interesting. I enjoyed it."

And then he went about putting groceries away and peeling and slicing two eggplants in preparation for the eggplant parmesan he planned to make for the next day's dinner. He stopped briefly to give me an affectionate hug and several kisses and to tell me how much he loved me and how fantastic life is.

I shook my head in mild disbelief, as I'd done so often during our years together. His ability to savor every aspect of life never ceased to amaze me, and I thought about what a joy he is to live with.

I went into my office and closed the door. I heard his familiar whistling. Ten minutes later he came in with a sumptuous chicken salad sandwich, a side dish of healthy salad, and a cup of tea flavored to my specifications. He paused just long enough to plant a kiss on the back of my neck. Then he left to work on the guest bathroom he'd been renovating.

I'd always thought of myself as an optimist, but I now understand that there's more to optimism than simply seeing the glass half full. Optimism is a mental attitude, a lifestyle. It's the ability to notice, absorb, and appreciate every waking moment—a feat I'd never believed was realistic. Until Marc.

He says he wasn't always this way. It took a decade for him to evolve into the person he is today—ten full years of anguish, heartache, and the grief of watching his beloved wife of forty-seven years succumb to Alzheimer's. He made a conscious decision to be happy. By his example, I am learning to rejoice in every moment.

REMINISCING

SOMETIMES I MISS CIGARETTES

C ountry singer Ronnie Dunn, of Brooks and Dunn, came out with an amazing song titled "I Wish I Still Smoked Cigarettes." The lyrics brought me back to an era that started when I was thirteen and fell deeply in love for the first time. Our relationship lasted from eighth grade through the middle of our sophomore year when family pressures insisted that it end. Our breakup has remained the most excruciating experience of my entire life. It was an innocent love—never more than sweet kisses. I miss what was never allowed to flourish, or die a natural death.

Dunn's song conjured up so many feelings and memories I'd forgotten. Sometimes I, too, wish I still smoked cigarettes. They signified so many pleasant things, such as independence and an exciting feeling of rebellion. A cigarette was something to look forward to at the end of dinner, when speaking on the phone and, of course, it was the pause that refreshed after making love.

I was fifteen and a sophomore in high school when I lit up my first one at my girlfriend's house. I can't recall which girlfriend, but I remember being surrounded by a group of friends cheering me on. I should have realized after my first drag that cigarettes were not my friends. I crumbled to the floor, landed on my friend's white shag rug, and lay there an undetermined amount of time, waiting for the room to stop spinning. Then I stood up and took a second drag.

In all other aspects of my life I was not a follower. In fact, I was a nauseatingly good girl. I couldn't bear the thought of displeasing my loving but strict parents. I followed all their rules. There were a great many, too, most of which began, "Good girls do this, and bad girls do that." Unlike most girls my age, I did not rebel. In retrospect I now know that a little rebelling may have been more difficult on my parents, but healthier—by far— for me.

I had dates every Friday, Saturday, and Sunday all through high school, and while that was great fun, I never experienced the kind of wild times many of my girlfriends did. I was far too busy rejecting boys' advances because good girls weren't permitted to have that kind of fun. My father said that a girl's reputation always arrived at a destination before she did, and it was that reputation by which she would be judged. I don't think a sullied reputation would have mattered very much to me, so I'm pretty sure I would do things differently today.

My mother used to hang up all the clothes I left piled on my bed and floor. My father told her not to pamper me, but she said, "Aw, Joe, she'll only be young once." She was wonderful, but he was right. I miss being spoiled.

I lived in New Jersey where the drinking age was eighteen. But just across the river, in Staten Island, the drinking age was seventeen. Every Saturday night piles of kids from Jersey schools drove to Staten Island to drink. I was never one of them. I miss never having gone with them.

Recently my ex-husband handed me a package of photos he knew I'd wanted for a long while. The pictures included ones of me in my mid-twenties. I was thrilled to have them, but as I sat staring at this pretty young girl with long, silky, brown hair, huge dark eyes, and a drop-dead figure, tears welled up. I barely recognized or remembered her and, God knows, I never fully appreciated her back then. Today my waist is thick, my breasts swing low, and I'm losing my battle with arthritis to stand erect.

So, yes, I sometimes miss cigarettes and periodically I revisit days gone by. I've come to realize it's not the cigarettes I miss so much as what they symbolize: all the other acts of teenage rebellion I never enjoyed because I was afraid to disappoint my parents.

Unfortunately, my children will never experience such regrets. They will have experienced everything.

WEDNESDAYS

Wednesday outings were therapeutic. They were my escape, my reward for having ignored my own needs the other six days of the week. On Wednesdays I kissed the children goodbye, watched them leave for school, washed the breakfast dishes, and ran to my car.

Solitude. At last.

In hot summer months Wednesdays found me escaping to Phillips Beach, fifty miles from home. It was a private beach at the Jersey Shore, minutes from Asbury Park. I arrived before it opened, at 9 a.m., lay on a beach blanket, let the hot summer sun warm my battered brain, and thought about ways to change my life. I spent hours swimming and jumping waves until the place closed at 6. Then I headed for Evelyn's, a seafood restaurant twenty minutes away in Belmar, before reluctantly heading home on the heavily trafficked Garden State Parkway.

Fall and winter, Wednesdays were spent in Manhattan, thirty-five minutes from home. I either hopped on a bus or drove into the city to see a Broadway show. I love the theater, and back in the seventies, for a mere seven dollars and fifty cents I enjoyed sensational shows such as *Pajama Game*, *The King and I*, *Tea and Sympathy*, *A Chorus Line*, *Sweeney Todd*, and *Chicago*. At the end of a play I left the theater, walked down the block to another theater box office, and purchased a ticket for the following week's performance. Over the years ticket prices hiked to nine, twelve, then twenty dollars and higher. Before long weekly trips to Broadway were out of my financial comfort range. My sensibilities forced me to go less frequently.

Sometimes I opted to drive into the city. I parked my car about three blocks from the theater in an underground parking garage off 42nd Street, a section noted back then for XXX-rated movies, peep shows, drugs, prostitutes, and fleabag rooms rented by the hour. I was never comfortable walking down 42nd Street, but I'd learned that if my stride was purposeful and confident, and I was careful not to make eye contact, odds were I wouldn't be robbed, raped, or murdered. There was always the occasional wolf whistle, or wise guys with comments such as, "Hey baby, here I am. Come and get it." One time a foul-smelling degenerate with tattered jeans, soiled T-shirt, greasy hair, and infestations on his face attempted to win me over by walking two feet in front of me, backwards, pledging his love for me, and reciting a list of obscenities he thought we might enjoy doing together. He was hard to ignore but I looked right through him and restrained my impulse to barf. The promise of seeing a Broadway show made those hazards bearable.

One day, after a show, I headed for my car when my left knee suddenly went out and I found myself facedown, eating the sidewalk. That knee had given me trouble since I was fourteen years old when I attempted to pick up and carry my boyfriend. We both fell to the ground. He was unscathed but I'd torn the cartilage in my left knee, which had been the source of many embarrassing but memorable stories ever since.

At my senior prom, where Louis Prima and Keely Smith were entertaining, I was jitterbugging with my date, Mike, when my knee went out. I landed facedown on the dance floor, humiliated. My date leaned over to help me up, but Prima stopped the band and came running down to me. He extended his hand, smiled, and said, "Nobody lies down when I'm on stage."

Another time, I was on a date in Manhattan. As was fashionable then, I was dressed in heels, gloves, and a white, off-the-shoulder sundress. As we crossed the street to Mamma Leone's, a well-known Italian restaurant, my knee went out, and I slid across the street on my stomach, through a mud puddle, narrowly missing getting hit by a taxi.

So there I was once again, facedown in the heart of Sin City. It mightn't have been so bad had I been wearing jeans and tennis shoes but I was wearing a beige suit with a pencil skirt. The skirt was hiked up so far, there was little doubt what color underwear I was wearing. My mother had always said to wear nice underwear in case of an accident. I wasn't sure whether it counted as an accident if a car wasn't involved, but I know she would have been proud because I was wearing lacy white panties, a fact to which everyone on that street corner could attest.

I was in pain, embarrassed, and feeling very unladylike. I tried to get up but couldn't. My knee had locked in a bent position. To move it was excruciating.

Staring down at me were two terrifying men, each eight feet tall. At least they were from my vantage point. One, I'm certain, was a pimp. He wore a sombrero-size purple hat, edged in leopard. His purple suit jacket had a shoulder span the width of a Volkswagen, and his pegged pants led straight to his pointed, purple, patent leather shoes.

The other one, a Mr. T clone, was menacing. He stood hovering over me, arms crossed over his chest, legs spread apart. His hair was shaved from his ears up, with only a two-inch span of it on top, and that was brushed into a point. It looked like the hair on a Kewpie doll I had as a child. The front of his T-shirt was ripped into a V, down to his navel, and the sleeves had been ripped off, probably during some violent activity. He wore about ten thick gold chains and massive gold rings that, I'm sure, also served as brass knuckles. He was Herculean.

I hoped they couldn't sense my terror.

Mr. T spoke.

"Ya' need help, lady?"

"No. Thank you. I'll be alright. I'm just having a little trouble standing."

"Le' me help ya'." He reached down for me.

"No, really. I can do it." I tried to turn onto my side, but the pain was sharp. I winced.

"Here, lady." He stooped down to help. "Take my arm."

"Let me try again." Please don't kill me. Please don't kill me. I tried, but the pain was unbearable. I was at his mercy.

Without saying a word, he reached down and scooped me up into his arms.

"Where's yer car?"

I hesitated, struggling with thoughts of being robbed, raped, or murdered, but I wasn't able to think of another solution.

"About two blocks down, in an underground garage," I answered. "You really don't have to do this."

In the midst of my terror a totally preposterous thought crept into my mind. I had recently put on several pounds and felt embarrassed that I might be too heavy for him to carry all the way to the car. He was sweating. It was a hot day.

The two-block walk happened in slow motion. I didn't know what protocol was. Should I attempt to make small talk about the show I'd just seen, or compliment him on his beautiful gold jewelry or his massive muscles? The quiet was deafening.

We finally arrived at my car. Still in his arms, and in pain, I leaned over and put my key into the door. He pulled the door open and placed me in the driver's seat, ever so gently, closed the door, turned, and walked away. My heart was pounding. I couldn't believe it. I was alive and intact.

I rolled down my window, waved a ten-dollar bill, and shouted, "Wait! Please come back. I want you to have this. I'm so grateful for your help."

He didn't turn around. He continued walking, raised his arm, and gestured a Queen Elizabeth wave.

I sat in my car a good five minutes, breathing heavily, waiting for my heart rate to slow down, and thinking about what a terrible person I was for having judged this man simply by the way he looked. I wasn't proud of myself.

I started the engine and headed for New Jersey; grateful for this wonderful Prince Charming, wondering what I would have done had he not been there to rescue me, and thankful that I'd injured my left leg. If I'd injured my right one, I couldn't have driven home, reported to my family, then gone directly to Saint Barnabas Hospital for torn meniscus surgery.

MOTHERS ON ICE

The manager of my son's hockey cub in 1978 asked me to participate in an exhibition game against mothers of the Canadian team my sons played annually.

I refused.

I was a horrible skater, easily distracted by everything, such as other people on the ice.

"You don't have to be good," he begged. "Two mothers haven't skated in ten years. One has never skated without the aid of someone's arm. One only skates clockwise, and none of the women know how to stop. Intentionally."

I qualified.

Practice, according to Webster, is a systematic exercise for proficiency. By definition we should have been refining existing skills, but we had none.

Our first practice was spent learning rules. At our second practice we reviewed fundamentals: how to remain vertical, how to fall without breaking bones, and how to get up before the end of any given period. Third and fourth sessions consisted of exercises and scrimmages and skating in large and small circles, counter and clockwise. We took shots on goal, practiced handling the stick and passing the puck until, quite literally, I could stand no more.

While several capable individuals emerged, we were terrible as a team.

The big night arrived. Juggling cumbersome hockey equipment under my arms, in both hands, and from my teeth, I backed in through the swinging doors of South Mountain Arena. I was not prepared for the mind-boggling crowd of more than four thousand that filled every corner of the place. I felt an overwhelming urge to flee. What had I gotten myself into? Was I prepared to make a complete fool of myself?

Most of us hadn't developed the knack of putting on layers of unwieldy protective equipment. So someone invariably put on stockings and skates, only to remember they'd forgotten their shin guards. We inadvertently put on shirts, suspenders, and pants before shoulder pads. Modesty was disregarded as husbands' flashbulbs and smiles lit up the locker room.

At the start of the game we were informed the Canadian team was short a couple of players, so we made the grand gesture of handing over two of our best. Everything's relative.

They were still short a goalie, so we watched as they dragged a Canadian spectator from the bleachers and positioned her, without skates, in front of their net. The only action she saw was between periods when her teammates lifted her by the elbows and deposited her in front of the opposite net. I remember thinking she should have brought something to read.

We slipped, fell, overshot goals, and misplaced the puck, all while struggling to maintain our dignity.

They looked professional. We looked ridiculous. The audience loved it. They cheered, whistled, squealed with delight, and applauded every second of play. I think they thought we were an act. Sadly, we weren't.

Carole, a first liner, made a rapid graceful entrance onto the ice, got the tip of her figure skate stuck in the ice (the opposition wore actual hockey skates), tripped over her own foot, fell, and was carried off the ice—all within the opening minute of the game.

Another mother, Debra, wore a red wig to keep from being recognized, thereby humiliating her family. She astonished everyone by making a goal and blowing her anonymity when the announcer shouted her name over the PA system.

I played defense. As I stood facing the opposition, frozen with terror, they repeatedly charged me, causing me to spin around and around as their puck flew past me and into our net.

We outnumbered them twenty-five to seven. We wore heavy protective uniforms; they sported fashionable, color-coordinated pantsuits. We changed lines every two minutes to avoid physical collapse; they only had one line.

We, the Livingston Zambunnies, were decidedly outranked by the Ville Emard Pussycats, who won by a huge margin—a number I choose to omit. Our only defense was the fact that they'd been playing as a team for many years, something we should have realized when we saw them remove their teeth at the start of the game.

Our goal of further cementing relations with our friendly Canadian competitors had surpassed our expectations. We pledged to continue the tradition.

CYBER SEDUCTION

P icture two strangers in cyberspace, letting their fingers do the talking, becoming closer with every keystroke, revealing things to each other they might never have the courage to say so early in a face-to-face relationship.

We probably all know someone who has experienced the seduction of getting to know a person through a dating site or chat room. There's something alluring about talking to a faceless stranger.

I've had several such experiences. The first time was when, after months of contemplating the idea, I finally succumbed to entering a chat room. I had entered one once before, but as a voyeur. I didn't have the chutzpah to cut into any of the swift-moving conversations rushing down my screen. I was too nervous to interrupt ongoing dialogue between people who, obviously, knew each other well. I didn't know where to jump in, what to say, or to whom I should direct my opening words.

Finally, I did it.

"Hello. I'm new at this so I need help on protocol," I wrote, signing myself Newtothis.

At first I was ignored and felt ridiculous. Then, one by one, responses came through.

"Hi, Newtothis. Welcome aboard. Just follow the conversation and break in anytime. Where are you from?"

"Northwest Jersey. How about you?"

"I'm from LA."

"Really? I have a number of friends and relatives there."

Eventually, the ice was broken and I found myself conversing, primarily with one guy. Before long our conversation was humming. His name was Richard and he enjoyed writing, as did I. An Army brat, he had traveled extensively, and he loved music and art. We had a great deal in common.

After about an hour he suggested we move to a private room. I had no idea what he was talking about, but by then he had captured my interest, so I let him take over. I learned that a private room was one where others were not privy to our one-on-one conversation.

Eventually he asked, "How old are you?"

"That's not something you ask a lady in the first few minutes of meeting her. LOL"

"Why not?" he asked. "I'm twelve."

I froze and audibly gasped.

How could that have happened? Not only had I been communicating with a seventh-grader, but the conversation had been so stimulating that I allowed him to take me into a private chat room. Was this the outcome of his supreme intelligence or a consequence of my extreme stupidity?

After I caught my breath and regained composure, I wrote, "I'm considerably older than you are, Richard, but it's been really great talking with you."

"WAIT!" he wrote. "Don't sign off. Please. I love older women."

I ignored his pleas and never entered another chat room.

After a reasonable period of recuperation, I did check out some dating sites and eventually married a man I met on AmericanSingles.com. My brief experience with Richard had not been in vain. I remembered the wisdom of not revealing one's age right away.

And then I reeled him in.

OOPS!

IN "LOO" OF GOOD TASTE

I shudder to think how my parents would have survived in to-day's anything-goes, nothing-is-sacred, sexually charged so-ciety. Their values were black and white, wrong and right, good and bad, with little wiggle room for compromise. My fa-ther banned me from the television when Elvis started his hip gyrations on the Ed Sullivan Show, so I'm certain he would not have endured today's reality shows and television commercials about incontinence, constipation, menstruation, toilet paper, and erectile dysfunction. Truth be known, I'm not doing so well, either.

Included on my list of "Things I Could Have Lived With-out" is information I acquired from a show about famous peo-ple found dead in their bathroom. Elvis and Catherine the Great are two. Given the many hours I spend in my bathroom, I was struck with the chilling thought that my final moments could be on a cold, tile floor.

I read somewhere that older people spend a lot of time in that room. Only now do I understand why. I have to pluck chin and mustache hair that I never had before. I have to dole out pills, too, which requires time and concentration. I never want to repeat the mistake of mixing up my morning diuretic and my evening sleeping pill, which had me sleeping all day and peeing all night. Also, the simple act of applying makeup now includes spackling my upper lip crevasses with a putty knife. These acts are all time consuming.

I summoned my husband.

"You know how much time I spend in the bathroom, right?"

He rolled his eyes.

"Yes, dear. I'm well aware."

"Promise that if you find me dead on the bathroom floor with my pants draped around my ankles, you'll pull 'em up or pull 'em off."

His eyes narrowed.

"You're not serious, are you?"

"I do not want to be found in an unladylike position. I want you to drag me into the bedroom and hoist me onto the bed and under the covers. Then place my arms on my chest, with a book—preferably something by Shakespeare or Tolstoy. Better yet, the Bible. Then you have to pluck any chin hairs you see. And you must do all this before you call 911."

His jaw dropped.

"Please put my mind to rest by promising you'll do this for me."

"You do know you're certifiable, right?"

Maybe, but aging brings to mind a variety of such preoccupations. Take adult diapers. Some people make fun of them. Even I have. But an incident occurred while we vacationed that has me thinking I won't do that anymore.

Our resort was so enormous that shuttles were provided to transport us to every campus venue: restaurants, pools, shopping, nightspots. Once we reached our destination a fair amount of walking was often required, so we brought along my fifty-pound, collapsible, battery-run wheelchair.

One evening we had just seen a wonderful Cirque du Soleil production, and were waiting with a number of others for the shuttle to arrive. When it pulled up Mighty Marc collapsed the wheelchair, placed it on the shuttle, and we each found a seat. I ended up alongside a young couple who looked to be in their late twenties.

The young man had watched Marc load my wheelchair. He turned to me and said in a voice loud enough for everyone to hear, "My grandma is cool. Nothing stops her from doing anything she wants. She's one busy old lady. She just straps on a diaper and heads for the mall. She never has to stop to take a leak. She just pisses her pants and keeps on goin', like the Energizer bunny."

For more than a month I was unable to get the picture of his grandma out of my head. If this is what the younger generation envisions when they see me actively enjoying life, I don't think I'll ever leave the house again.

BATHROOM FiASCOES

received a ten-dollar coupon for my favorite shoe store. I left the store $329 lighter than when I entered. I know that sounds like an awful lot of money, but when you consider that I hadn't bought shoes in four years, it doesn't seem so bad. I'd not purchased shoes, which I love nearly as much as I love my husband (okay, just a teensy bit more), because of a bunion, a hammertoe, an arthritic back, two knee replacements, and one hip replacement, all of which make walking painful in anything but slippers.

But some brilliant shoe designers have been paying attention. They're designing shoes for the Senior Generation. Along with a huge variety of elegant, I-would-kill-to-be-able-to-wear, pencil-thin spikes, there were countless shelves of flats.

Don't get me wrong. Flats can never replace glamorous heels that make even piano legs look slim, graceful, and sexy but, for the first time in years, I actually had a decent selection to select from.

There I was, pushing my walker up and down the aisles, stopping every five feet to try on another pair, when I needed a bathroom break. I found my way to the restroom and pushed open the door. The room was pitch dark. I slid my hand over the wall, feeling for the light switch, when—without any help from me—the lights went on automatically.

I found a stall. Because I was exhausted, I decided to give my legs a rest and hang out a few minutes. Suddenly, the lights went out.

It was déjà vu. Just three weeks earlier, I'd found myself in the same situation in a restaurant restroom. No one was there but me. I had assumed there was an outage. It was a long, large bathroom and I couldn't see a thing. I felt my way along the wall to the door, opened it, and was surprised to see the restaurant lights were still on. Apparently, the woman who had exited the bathroom before me had turned out the lights, either out of habit or with mischievous intent.

So there I sat in the shoe store restroom, in pitch darkness, not sure I could even find my way to the sink. By then I realized some great decision maker up the chain of command had determined how long the average individual should take in the bathroom and set a timer. I, apparently, had overstayed my welcome.

I found the sink and washed my hands. As my eyes adjusted to the darkness, I couldn't believe what I saw. At first I thought it might be some kind of a bidet, but it was too low to the floor, possibly for use by pygmies only.

Gradually, I realized it was a urinal. OMG! I had been lingering in a men's bathroom. I'd even been casual enough to take a few moments to freshen my lipstick. It was by the grace of God that a man hadn't walked in.

I found the door, pushed it open, and exited, grateful no one was around to have witnessed my screwup.

Several weeks later I was in the restroom at our local diner. Before returning to my table, I did my wiggle dance, which consists of hunching my shoulders, grabbing on to the lower part of my bra and wiggling, to adjust and realign my girls. When I got to the sink I was shocked to see a middle-aged man washing his hands and looking into the mirror. I didn't want to embarrass him, but I couldn't think of a thing to say or do that wouldn't bring about that result.

"Excuse me," I smiled. "I think you're in the wrong restroom." My statement didn't seem to register. He continued washing his hands and didn't acknowledge my words or my presence. So I repeated myself. "Excuse me, I'm pretty sure you're in the wrong restroom."

Suddenly, his head swiveled like Linda Blair's in the Exorcist as he rapidly viewed all corners of the room and then me.

"Jesus Christ!" he gasped as he turned and flew out the door.

I'm fairly certain his feet never touched the ground.

I'd love to have heard the whopper he told his buddies.

EMBARRASSiNG REALiTY CHECK

We were in Connecticut, visiting our son, Andy, and his family. We'd made a large purchase at Ace Hardware store. Marc and I remained at the cash register as my son walked to the other side of the room to discuss delivery date details with the salesperson.

When I looked down I saw my son had left his wallet on the counter. I took his wallet, put it into my coat pocket, and said to Marc, "Andy has to learn to be more mindful of what he's doing. When he goes to look for it, he'll get a scare."

We walked out of the store. He still didn't notice his wallet was missing, so I held out my hand, smiled, and gave it to him. He took it and made some kind of excuse about having been all wrapped up in conversation with the salesman.

I was feeling smug.

We were on the road around ten minutes when his cell phone rang. He took the call, said "Thank you," and hung up.

"That was the hardware store," he said. "You left your pocketbook on the counter."

IT'S HOW DEEP?

My mother and I were close. We spoke on the phone every day, not out of obligation but out of love. We always had something interesting or funny to report. Her life was full, as was mine, but we managed to get together for lunch every couple of weeks.

She was a beautiful woman in every way. Heads turned when she passed. Older men looked. Young ones, too. There was something about her that attracted everyone. She had a rare and wonderful combination of stately elegance and child-like naïveté. You never saw her without a smile on her face. She was sweet. She was kind, and she was loved by everyone who met her.

When she turned sixty-two my brother, Wayne, and I threw a surprise birthday party for her. It was a large party at my house with good food, good music, and a gypsy fortune-teller who we later discovered had reported terrible "truths" to guests, including upcoming diseases and deaths.

I hand drew the invitation, which was a caricature of my mother. It was a simple line drawing of her face that depicted her two outstanding features—large almond-shaped eyes, which she accentuated with long black false eyelashes, and big blonde hair that swept behind her left ear and swooped into a deep wave above her right eye. It was a glamorous hairdo and quite flattering to the shape of her face though it hadn't been popular since Veronica Lake sported a version of it back in the

1940s. In the late 1970s it was noticeably outdated, but because my mother was such a fashion icon, it became her signature. Being the exquisite beauty she was, she carried it off with elegance and aplomb.

My mother loved the sun. If she passed a mirror and didn't like what she saw, she'd say, "I'm ready for a tan." She circled the world four times with the goal of getting a tan on every continent. And when, heaven forbid, she couldn't get away from harsh New Jersey winters, she ventured out to her backyard in the bitter cold. There she sat in a beach chair under layers of heavy blankets with an aluminum reflector tilted to catch and intensify the sun's rays. I scolded her, reminding her that too much sun would make her look old and wrinkled.

"I'm sixty-five," she replied. "If I can't have wrinkles at my age, when can I have them? A tan will enhance them."

When she wasn't on some tropical island, my mother enjoyed the Jersey Shore, where she walked to the sea's edge, bent over, and gently splashed water over her legs, arms, and chest. But at no time, and I mean never, did my mother allow her hair to get wet. I couldn't understand why she felt the need to be cautious. Her hair was so heavily lacquered there was no doubt it was impervious to all forms of moisture. But she chose not to take a chance.

One steamy day as she and I lay basking in the sun at a posh Florida resort, she spotted a woman in the pool. The woman stood in water that came midway between her elbows and shoulders. My mother, who by then was in desperate need of a dunk, raised herself from her chaise lounge and approached the woman.

"Excuse me. The water doesn't look terribly deep here," she said. "Are you touching the bottom?"

"Oh, yes, I'm standing here with no trouble," the woman assured her. Then she turned and swam away.

Anxious to cool off, my mother sat on the edge of the pool. Slowly and carefully, she slipped her body into the water and proceeded to drop down, down, down, well over her head. I jumped up from my lounge chair to see if she had drowned.

Gasping and wildly thrashing her arms, she returned to the surface and latched onto the side of the pool. Her lacquered bouffant hairstyle had maintained its original shape, just as I had always suspected it would. Each hair stayed obediently glued in its original location. The only difference was that it had shifted, en masse, to one side.

My mother dragged herself up the ladder. I'm quite certain I saw flames of rage shoot from her nostrils as she plopped into her lounge chair and quickly wrapped her deflated hair in a large beach towel. This was a woman who had never even allowed her husband to see her without perfectly coiffed hair.

It was several moments before she said anything. I heard her hyperventilating as her eyes narrowed and she scanned the pool for the "bitch" who had deceived her. She spotted her, walking in our direction.

As the woman came closer, my mother prepared to stand and lash out at her. Suddenly, though, she stopped and lowered herself back down into the lounge chair. Her facial expression softened. Her shoulders relaxed. It all made sense. The woman was over six feet tall.

My mother was five foot four.

FUN AS iN FUNERAL

F riends are keeling over like dominoes. Every time one dies I run to my mirror, hoping to find something that will confirm I'm still too vibrant to go into the fertilizer business.

The first time a friend died was a rude awakening. I was inconsolable. She had been a lifetime friend. My sorrow intensified as I pondered the fact that she was my peer, and I was way too young to be the same age as someone who died of old age.

Wasn't I?

Every time I'm faced with another funeral I get the same argument from my husband.

"I don't want to go," he says. "I didn't even know him. He was your friend."

"We don't go to funerals for the deceased," I say. "We go for the living."

"Well, I don't like funerals."

"You're kidding, right? That's hard to believe. Most people love them."

I usually end up going alone.

I was in the funeral parlor seated alongside my newly widowed friend, Sheila. She and Stewart had what she described as a fairy-tale marriage. They had never spent a night apart. (That wheezing you hear is me, suffocating.) Their fifty-four-year marriage yielded eight children, which is bound to happen if you never spend a night apart.

We were about six feet from the open casket. Guests walked up and offered condolences. People are often uncomfortable doing this, as one woman proved.

"I was so sorry to learn about Stewart's passing," she said. "I just looked at him and I have to say I've never seen him look so bad."

Seriously? The man was room temperature and she didn't think he looked well?

After funeral services we were invited back to Sheila's home to sit Shiva. During this time people drop by to pay respect, share warm stories about the deceased, and eat. Show me a Jewish event of any kind, and I'll show you an excuse to eat.

One young woman suffered from foot-in-mouth disease as she babbled on about the previous night's episode of The Simpsons. At the end of a lengthy spiel that had her laughing hysterically as she related details of the show, she turned to my grieving friend and asked, "Did you see The Simpsons last night?"

Loud silence.

I was relieved to learn that the mentally ill aren't the only ones who laugh at a funeral. I was at my brother's gravesite. Wayne and I had been close. As part of the traditional Jewish service, I was handed a shovel, dug into the fresh mound of earth alongside his resting place, and spread the soil over his lowered casket. This represents the final act one can do for a loved one to see him off safely. It was the saddest moment of my life, but instead of crying I heard myself giggle. I was horrified. I was thinking about something that had occurred at our mother's funeral four years earlier.

I'd worn a colorful, handcrafted silk shawl. Wayne sported an expensive designer tie. The rabbi approached us, recited a prayer, and with the speed and skill of Edward Scissorhands, he cut a small gash into my shawl and Wayne's tie. To assure that they couldn't possibly be repaired, he then tugged at each cut, which produced ragged, frayed edges. This act is called Kriah and represents grief and anger over the loss of a loved one. Some rabbis choose to give mourners a small, torn, black ribbon to pin over their hearts, but our rabbi favored destroying our garments beyond repair.

In the presence of countless puzzled mourners, Wayne and I looked blankly at each other and, inappropriately, laughed. We later decided it was a coping mechanism; the result of a buildup of grief and stress.

My husband is eighty years old, looks sixty, and feels fifty. He's physically and mentally active. While he makes long-term plans as though he's going to live forever, I keep checking my watch to see how many minutes I have left. And, while he plays golf, chops down trees, and adds a porch onto our house, I'm in doctors' offices, operating rooms, and physical therapy, which leaves little time or energy for the jitterbugging and sky-diving I'd planned to do at this age.

The next time someone glibly tells me, "You're only as old as you feel," I can't promise I won't smack him over the head with my cane. But first I'll ask if he's talking about mentally or physically because mentally, I'm in my thirties, but physically, I'm circling the drain.

WATER, WATER, EVERYWHERE

When I turned on the hot water, it spit at me. For no reason I could understand, water and air sputtered in short angry gulps, then spit at me.

Of course I realized this was not normal behavior for water, but I was not up to dealing with it. So I ignored it.

The spitting and sputtering continued, day in and day out, for six days. I was still in denial. Since only my hot water was displaying weird symptoms, I reasoned the problem was not contagious. If it was, the cold water would have already caught it.

Then, exactly seven days from the first time it happened I awoke, staggered into the bathroom in my usual morning stupor, turned on the water and ... nothing. No sputtering. No spitting. No water.

I have a well in back of my house. At least that's what the house inspector had told me eight years earlier when I moved in. I have no way of knowing whether he told me the truth as I've never seen it. My only proof is that I don't get water bills. Just then terror shot through me as I considered the possibility that there actually was a well back there—and it had dried up.

I ran for the phone. My plumber arrived promptly, checked my electrical breakers, crawled into the cubby under my basement stairs, and scratched his head. A half dozen tests and tools later, my water pump was pronounced dead.

What, exactly, did "dead" mean? What had killed it? And, most important, what would this cost me?

The pump had to be dug up and replaced. Clutching my heart with one hand and my checkbook with the other, I watched as two men dug and dug and dug until they eventually located whatever they were looking for. This was followed by the burdensome extraction and unfurling of what seemed like several miles of piping that stretched diagonally from one corner of my property to the other. It was then they discovered the pump had not died a natural death. It had been struck by lightning.

I clearly remembered the electrical storm that had passed through the previous week. I'd managed to shut down everything electric in my all-electric house for a period of four hours. The plumber explained the lightning probably had originated a considerable distance from my house and had traveled underground to the pump. Since the pump is only about fifteen feet from my house, the thought frightened me, but my concerns rapidly vanished when he informed me the $1,300 I was preparing to fork over would be covered by insurance.

As I review my years in this house, it seems my life here has been ruled by water. Because of very hard water and a horrible sulfur odor, I went through two hot water heaters in a six-year period before the source of the problem was detected: an incompetent water softener. I had to replace it. I'd had three floods due to foreign particles clogging that new water softener. My washing machine flooded twice and, during a particularly horrible storm, water seeped through the tiles of my basement floor, causing a huge argument between me and my then-boyfriend. I'd started the cleanup process by laying down sheets of the Sunday New York Times, and he insisted the only way to sop up water was with towels.

I showed him by stomping out of the house in the dark of night, driving off into the storm, and getting stuck in a gully that gushed a foot of water into my car. The water swished back and forth across my feet. It rose up into my glove compartment where my car phone wires were located, disabling the phone I'd purchased for just such emergencies.

I love water and have always dreamed of living surrounded by it—but I meant a lake, creek, pond, or river. Obviously, the Powers That Be misunderstood.

BELiEVE iT AND YOU WiLL SEE iT

A number of years ago a North Carolina cousin chose Phoenix, Arizona as his wedding destination. Our huge extended family was only too happy to fly in, from all points, and celebrate with him. We're a close-knit family and being together guarantees laughter and a terrific time.

At one point my cousin Myra and I wandered off by ourselves to sightsee and shop. I rented a gold Chrysler convertible, and we drove up and down the main thoroughfare and over the steep back hills. Several wrong turns found us in areas we hadn't planned on visiting, but it was an adventure and we loved it.

We stopped for lunch at a lovely hotel high in the hills. From our seats on the patio we enjoyed a breathtaking, panoramic view of the red canyon.

On our way out of the hotel we stopped at the gift shop and giggled like teenagers as we tried on an array of hats. I found one I liked, but the price was exorbitant. It was brown straw, with a wide brim, a beaded turquoise and silver headband, and chin strap. Usually hats make me look ridiculous but I looked pretty good in that one.

"Buy it, Laverne," Myra encouraged. "You look great."

"It's too expensive," I said. "I have no right spending that much money on anything, much less a hat I'll probably never wear once I leave Arizona."

"What are you talking about?" she asked. "You can afford it. You have more than enough money to last you the rest of your life."

I cocked my head. She seemed more confident and knowledgeable than I did on the subject.

"I do?"

"Yes," she said, smiling impishly, "provided you die within the next three months."

I bought the hat and wore it the entire four days I was there. Then I took it home and hung it on the wall in my den, as part of the existing southwestern design.

Extravagant? Yes. But I never regretted it.

Roughly seven years later, I was in Arizona again. It was a different kind of vacation for me. Generally, a vacation that makes me happy includes a body of water, lounge chairs, and tall drinks with umbrellas. This time I was with my husband. We had chosen Scottsdale because it's known for art galleries and southwestern pottery, and we were on a mission to find items to decorate our newly renovated home.

We walked through countless small shops and galleries. I wanted everything. Mighty Marc had to physically restrain me on more than one occasion.

Then I saw it: a beautiful bright red and orange handblown rectangle, roughly 2′ x 2½′, set in swirls of black wrought iron. It was meant to hang on a wall. My wall. We agreed it was perfect for our television room so we bought it and paid to have it shipped.

We were back in New Jersey about three weeks when we decided to hang the piece on our wall. Mighty Marc went into the bedroom to get it from where we'd stored it, under the bed. It wasn't there, and that surprised us. We looked in closets, in the basement, and in the attic. We were completely baffled because we both remembered that when the piece was delivered, we had shoved it under the master bed for safekeeping.

We sat on the living room couch, scratching our heads, bewildered, trying to figure out where we'd put it. It wasn't as though we were attempting to track down a box of chocolate truffles or a bottle of Merlot. We would have known where they went.

Just then someone knocked on the front door. It was a FedEx man with a package. We signed for it, ripped it open, and turned to each other in disbelief. There it was, the glass sculpture we'd been searching for. The sculpture we clearly remembered as having been delivered. The sculpture we both recalled pushing under the bed. That it should be delivered at that moment magnified the absurdity of the situation.

It would have been weird enough if only one of us was certain the sculpture had already been delivered, but the fact that it involved us both was downright mystifying, not to mention bizarre.

Marc laughed the whole thing off, but I found that difficult to do. Either evil forces were at work that afternoon, or we were both fading into senility at the same rate of speed.

I wasn't sure which to hope for.

I QUIT

W hile watching a reality cooking competition, I found myself salivating. I thought how rewarding it would be to create a delectable concoction. Then I remembered how much I hate to cook and switched channels.

I used to love cooking. I owned dozens of cookbooks. If a recipe looked appealing, I rarely followed it. Instead I made a note of the main ingredients, then added or subtracted ingredients to suit my own taste. When guests said, "You must give me that recipe," I couldn't. I've never been able to make the same thing twice.

Mighty Marc enjoys cooking, but his style is the antithesis of mine. He is a purist. If the recipe should happen to say, "With your hands go clap, clap, clap. With your feet go tap, tap, tap," he would not stop to question it. Rather, he would put down his wooden mixing spoon and start clapping and tapping. Why? Because "that's what the recipe calls for."

I used to be an excellent cook, but my casual, unorthodox style qualifies me as the world's worst baker. Baking requires precise measurements and patience. I hate precision, and I have no patience. I even failed at baking a Betty Crocker boxed cake mix because I applied frosting to the cake before it cooled, which resulted in a pile of crumbs. It tasted great but looked like clumps of yellow play dough. Knowing my guests were entitled to dessert, I scooped piles of cake chunks onto each person's dish and passed around the cake mix box so they could see a picture of what they were eating.

Several years back I entered a Jersey Fresh statewide cooking contest. There were only two rules: I had to create the recipe, and it had to include vegetables grown in New Jersey. My casual guess-and-toss cooking style wouldn't work. I needed accurate measurements. So I dusted off my measuring utensils and forced myself to record everything. My psyche operates better with spontaneity than precision, so this measuring was extremely difficult for me. Fairly satisfied that I'd guessed correctly, I mailed in the recipe with my entry form.

I was stunned when Jersey Fresh phoned to say that, out of hundreds of entries, I'd been selected, with nine others, to come to Atlantic City and prepare my recipe in some big hotel. The judges would be a group of renowned chefs and newspaper food critics.

I was accustomed to cooking on an electric stove. The hotel had gas burners the size of manhole covers that totally intimidated me. As it happened, I came in third, won three hundred dollars, and had some great newspaper, radio, and television publicity.

In light of how cooking was once an important part of my life, it saddens me that I no longer derive any joy from it at all. Cooking for company has become difficult. It was more fun when my only concerns were that it tasted good and I made enough.

I recently invited a group over for an afternoon barbecue. I was looking forward to it until the phone calls started coming in. One person didn't eat meat. One had a peanut allergy. One only ate fish. One said garlic upset her stomach. Two were gluten free. One was a vegetarian. Two were lactose intolerant. One only ate white meat chicken.

They arrived with Benadryl, probiotics, Lactaid, EpiPens and, in one case, her own food. The world was more fun when everyone was ignorant, and I could serve anything from one of

Paula Deen's cookbooks without the need for apologies and a side of Lipitor.

I've had it with cooking. I've cooked more than sixty thousand meals in my lifetime and I now know I can be happy if I never set foot in my kitchen again.

The late, great comedian Totie Fields said that when she got married she told her husband, "I can only be good in one room. You pick the room." Consequently, she never had to cook. I'm going to dress in something seductive and make that same offer to Mighty Marc, but I'm a little nervous that at our age he might opt for the wrong room.

EAVESDROPPING

LET'S TRADE PLACES FOR A MOMENT

I was sitting in my favorite Japanese restaurant, alone, doing the two things I love most: eating sushi and eavesdropping. Two men, probably in their mid-fifties, were seated in a booth behind me, discussing their mothers. Their conversation was so absorbing that I grabbed pen and pad from my purse and began taking notes.

"She drives me crazy," said Son #1. "She calls every fucking day, complaining that I don't call. I asked what difference it makes who does the calling if we communicate every day? But she wants me to call her. And each time we speak, she needs a full report of that day's activities. I dread hearing the phone ring. I mean—I love her, but I don't have time for this crap. She needs to get a life."

"That's gotta be tough on you," said Son #2. "I guess she's lonely since your dad died."

"She plays bridge on Wednesdays, and the senior bus takes her to the market once a week, so I doubt she's lonely."

Every woman's fantasy life.

"Does she drive?"

"No more. Her eyesight isn't great, so after she had a near miss on the road, we took her keys. She wasn't happy about it."

"Hey, I get it. What choice did you have?"

Touch my car keys and you're dead.

"She'd like to move to a senior retirement community. The one she wants is fifty minutes away. Too far. Besides, I hear a lot of hanky-panky goes on in those places. Not really the environment I want my mother exposed to."

"Well, get this," said Son #2. "My mother, who's seventy-three, made a plane reservation for California. I can't get her to sit in one place for more than five minutes. She'll be traveling, cross-country, alone! And when she gets there, she'll be shacking up with an old boyfriend she reconnected with on Facebook, which makes me sick to think about. I'm damn sure they won't be playing Tiddlywinks. I wish to hell she'd act her age."

I stopped chewing.

What the hell did that mean? I've read books on what to expect from infants, toddlers, and teenagers, but, if there's one titled "Characteristics Commonly Found in Women Over Seventy," I missed it. And, by the way, dummy, it's not as if she'll be piloting the plane. She'll be securely seated in one place—for more than five minutes—which should thrill you. Furthermore, there's no expiration date on one's sex drive, so get over it.

I had all I could do to keep from turning around and poking him in the face with a chopstick.

"Does she have anything physically wrong that could prevent her from traveling alone?" asked Son #1.

"Not really. She has some arthritis in her back and she did have a hip replacement, but she says she's fine. Still, the woman's much too old to be traipsing around the country herself. I tried to talk her out of it but she blew me off."

By the time I finished eating, my head was throbbing. One son had neither empathy nor time for his lonely mother, who had become a pain in his sanctimonious ass. The other son would have been happy to contain his spirited mother within the confines of a fenced-in yard. Perhaps if he tossed her a pair of earphones and a bag of salted almonds, he could convince her she was in a plane.

How much easier both sons' lives would be without these burdensome women.

On my drive home I tried to see both sides. Was there any validity to what these men were saying? Was Mother #1 too clingy? Should she not lean so heavily on her son and aim at making a new life for herself? Had alternate forms of transportation been discussed when they removed her keys? Was her son's exasperation justified?

Was Son #2 reasonable in his attempt to frustrate his mother's travel plans? Should his worries take precedence over her desires? Were his negativity and criticism his way of showing loving concern, or did he, quite simply, resent having an additional thing to worry about?

It suddenly occurred to me that I might not be the right person to judge these men. My parents died young. Losing them left a huge hole in my heart. I missed out on the enjoyment of having an adult relationship with them. But I understood later in life that their deaths also freed me from the worries, demands, and exasperation that I might have experienced if I'd had to care for them.

I would hope that while adult children cope with aging parents, they take a moment to understand that the wrinkles on our faces and the canes we lean on are not indicative of who we are. We do not want to be viewed with pity, disdain, tolerance, or condescension. We don't want to be a burden. We ask only that you be patient and understand that while all of this is new for you, it's also new for us.

Please take time to talk and listen to us. You might be pleasantly surprised to find that we are witty, charismatic, well informed about a wide range of subjects, and still full of life. We ask that you discard your preconceived notions about our generation and be cognizant of the fact that one day, you will be us.

Equally important is, your children are watching. How you treat us will likely be how they treat you.

NOW HEAR THiS

ost seniors spend money doing things they didn't have time for, or couldn't afford, before they retired. Some use their retirement savings to play endless golf. Others buy boats, sports cars, gifts for their grandchildren, or go on cruises. My sin of choice is dining out—a lot. I once was an innovative, creative cook who derived joy from preparing gourmet meals for my family. But that was in my last life. Now I spend as little time as possible in the kitchen, other than to open the fridge for a swig of Hershey's chocolate syrup.

Eating out is fattening. A chef once told me that if he obeyed the cooking requests of dieters, the food would taste so horrendous, people would never return. So, if I order fish dry without sauce or butter, and it tastes delicious, it's not my fault if I enjoy it, even though I know it can't possibly be the dry piece of cardboard I ordered.

I justify the expense by telling myself that restaurants are a great source for writing material and, in fact, they are. I love to eavesdrop. I've learned a great deal listening to people who don't know I'm spying on them. I grabbed my pad and pen when I overheard a woman at a nearby table explaining to her dinner companion how she makes papier-mâché puppets. Then I went home and tried it. What fun that was.

Another time I eavesdropped on a dogmatic, boisterous cretin who was preaching to his dinner companion that the Holocaust was no more than a well-polished newsreel. It's difficult to maintain decorum when listening to a knuckle-dragging twit.

Sunday, we went out for brunch. We enjoy reading the paper while we eat. Mighty Marc put coins in the newspaper machine outside the diner, opened it, and reached for a Sunday New York Times.

"Holy @$#!" he said, nearly losing his balance while lifting the fifty-pound newspaper.

Just then he noticed a couple walking out of the diner.

"Jeez, do you think they heard me curse?" he asked.

"I'm sure they did," I answered. "But it's Sunday, so maybe they thought you were praying."

Once we were in the diner, the waitress asked for my order. I couldn't decide what to eat, so I recited my laundry list of what I can't eat.

"Eggs have cholesterol. French toast has eggs. Pancakes have eggs. Ham, bacon, and sausage have cholesterol. Bread is a carbohydrate. Syrup and jelly are carbohydrates. Coffee has caffeine. Oatmeal won't kill me, but if I eat it once more this week, I'll barf."

Unfazed, she shifted from one leg to the other, pen poised over her pad.

"Bring me a package of soup oysters, a cup of hot water, and several slices of lemon."

"Will that be all?" she asked.

"No. Throw in a side of turkey sandwich on whole wheat toast."

"That comes with French fries or potato chips."

"You had to tell me that?" I whined. "If you'd have just slapped the plate down in front of me I'd have felt obliged to eat whatever was on it. Now I have to make a responsible decision, damn it!"

The waitress walked away with a head twitch I'd not noticed before.

We sat reading our paper when I remembered we were supposed to have defrosted chicken for that evening's meal. I looked at Mighty Marc.

"Did you take the chicken out before we left?" I asked.

"No, I thought you had."

The man in the booth behind Marc turned and looked at us, so I couldn't resist.

"I'd planned on doing that," I said, "but I couldn't find her leash."

I figure it's my duty to keep other eavesdroppers informed.

SEASONAL

JOY TO THE WORLD? SAYS WHO?

Christmas is approaching and I've not yet recuperated from last year. Truth is, I've been curled up on the floor of my closet in a fetal position, unable to face the inevitable. It's supposed to be a cheerful time of year. If asked to depict a typical holiday scene, most people would probably describe a smiling family sitting around the dining room table enjoying a festive Christmas dinner. Their vision might include children sitting cross-legged in front of a Christmas tree unwrapping gifts by a roaring fire while Fido struggles to remove an annoying red bow around his neck.

Unfortunately, I don't see Christmas that way anymore. Rather than face the insanity that the holiday brings, I would opt to be audited by the IRS in a dentist's chair during a root canal. Maybe I haven't expressed myself strongly enough: I would rather have George Clooney show up at my door with a box of chocolates and a bouquet of roses, and find me with cold cream smeared over my face, curlers in my hair, and a huge pimple on my nose.

I can hear your hisses and bah humbugs, but I can't help it. I don't know how to take on the added work and stress that holidays bring without becoming flustered, exhausted, emotionally depleted, and teary-eyed.

Some people find pleasure in writing gift lists, hunting for parking spaces in crowded malls, and battling crazed shoppers for the toy of the season. I've been told they even enjoy waiting in long lines at the cash register because it energizes them and puts them in the holiday spirit.

Not me.

Some delight in addressing scores of Christmas card envelopes, planning the holiday menu, cooking, baking, and hunting for decorations. They even like polishing silver, ironing tablecloths, creating centerpieces, shopping for presents, and decorating their home and the Christmas tree.

Uh-uh. Not me.

Trying to maintain sanity and a semblance of organization throughout the rest of the year is challenging enough. I put sticky notes on my headboard to remind me to change the sheets. I don't remember to go marketing until I discover there's nothing in my fridge except a container of sour milk and a "fur"-covered jello mold I forgot to serve at a party three months earlier. I'm so disorganized I create daily lists of things to do, then lose them. I make life-changing goals before going to bed and completely forget about them by sunrise. I show up at the doctor's office when I should be at the hairdresser. I arrive one week late for weddings. Add the Christmas holiday bedlam to my dysfunctional, hyperactive, overloaded brain and you're simply asking for more than it can handle.

For years I hosted Chanukah parties. Everyone enjoyed them. Then one of my sons married a Greek Orthodox girl, my daughter married a Catholic boy, and I found myself a nice Italian. Suddenly, more than one holiday had to be recognized. Normal hectic turned into sweaty pandemonium as a slew of new and unfamiliar traditions and responsibilities were added to my life. My tiny eight-inch Chanukah menorah sat in the shadow of a sparkling, six-foot Christmas tree. "I Have a Little Dreidel" was wedged between "White Christmas" and "Silent Night." Chicken soup with matzo balls preceded an antipasto, and brisket shared the spotlight with a spiral ham. I no longer had three children and five grandchildren to buy gifts for; I had eight children, nineteen grandchildren, and four great-grandchildren.

I want to be like my girlfriend, Adrienne. She has a handle on life. She can stand at her kitchen counter tearing romaine lettuce for a salad and talk to her guests at the same time, without beads of moisture forming on her forehead. I can never do that. When well-meaning guests insist on helping me in the kitchen, I have to bite my lip to keep from screaming, "Go away! I can't possibly slice this meatloaf and tell you where I keep plastic wrap at the same time."

This year I'm asking Santa for a new, uncluttered brain. The brain I've been using is stuffed to capacity. I want one that keeps me tranquil in the throes of chaos and allows me to find pleasure in the rituals, traditions, and insanity of the holiday season.

If he gives me that, I promise to be a good girl . . . until next holiday season when all bets are off.

NEXT YEAR I'M CANCELLING AUGUST

Life turned slightly sour this summer when we returned from a lovely five-day visit to my son and his family in Connecticut. Suitcase still in hand, we walked into our kitchen and stepped into a puddle in front of the refrigerator. Uh-oh. Upon further investigation we saw that frozen foods had turned to mush and milk didn't smell that great. Even though the motor was running, whatever makes a refrigerator cold had died and leaked.

We had no choice but to rush out and buy a new one. After comparison shopping at Sears, Lowe's, and Home Depot, we decided on a French Door bottom freezer refrigerator. It cost a fortune but we could have it delivered immediately.

I care for five outdoor cats. I had them each spayed. They show their appreciation by allowing me to feed them and leaving dead birds at my door. I have no idea how, but one cat, Midnight, broke her foot. It took over a week to trap her and bring her to the vet, who took X-rays, then told us she could not get the specific care she needed because she is an outdoor cat. She gave Midnight a shot for pain and handed her back to us, along with a bill for $400.

This would have been painful in and of itself, but on the way back we drove over a huge lug nut that punctured a hole the size of Rhode Island in our brand new expensive Michelin tire. Replacement and labor came to $230.

We were barely into the second week of August when I walked into our basement and spotted a puddle. This time it was from the hot water heater. In no time flat, we were the proud owners of a shiny new $500 hot water heater. I gave thought to hanging out a sign, "Puddles Are Us."

Right about this time Mighty Marc and I looked at each other with the same idea: Perhaps we should cancel our upcoming September vacation at a Canadian resort. We weren't sure we could trust our luck, or had the right to spend the money.

Several days later I went to the dentist for a routine checkup. My teeth were not bothering me at all but I know good oral hygiene is important. The dentist, my ex-husband, said my teeth were in good health.

"Oh, wait, there's a little pocket here that should be looked at by a periodontist," he said.

Fortunately, there was a periodontist right next door who rushed over, poked a long, sharp instrument hard and deep into my gums, and made them bleed. Then he said, "Your gums are bleeding." I knew he was telling the truth because I tasted blood running down my throat.

He said that if my gums were healthy, they would not bleed. I was dying to challenge that theory on him, but never got the opportunity. Fortunately (for him), he was able to perform the surgery on me immediately, after which he handed me a bill for $955, which I signed using the blood that was still dripping from my mouth.

I went to fill a prescription for an inhaler I had been using for twenty years and discovered it had been discontinued. But I could replace it with another one for a mere $142 for a thirty-day supply, which was triple what my other inhaler had cost.

We cancelled our Canadian vacation and mapped out a money-saving plan where we would each eat on alternate days. Then we plopped down in front of the TV, swaddled in Kevlar blankets, and waited for September.

Next year I'm cancelling August.

'TIS THE SEASON

Something nice happens every year just about the time that leaves and temperatures begin to fall and garden centers switch from selling strawberries and sweet corn to pumpkins and apples.

For women, it manifests itself in a sudden impulse to bake apple and pumpkin pies and knit mittens and afghans. Men hurry outdoors to cover deck furniture, chop firewood, and rake leaves, and find themselves actually enjoying it all.

The crisp air is filled with the scent of burning leaves and the promise of good things to come. Happy feelings escalate as vacant lots display Christmas trees and Santa's knee becomes every youngster's desired destination. Trips to the mall are frequent, hearts beat faster than usual, and our love for mankind intensifies.

Somewhere in the midst of these joyful feelings and fun-filled activities, disquieting facts and disturbing images cast dark shadows over our hearts. They appear as front-page newspaper stories that describe the plight of the homeless and include appeals for charitable holiday donations. They surface in photographs of children who look older than their years, with vacant expressions in their eyes, and no hope in their hearts—children who know better than to dream of American Girl dolls and electronic video games and pray only for warm coats and shoes with soles.

These stories deeply move us, so we write checks and pull children's name tags from huge mall Christmas trees and buy them gifts. Doing these charitable deeds mollifies our desire to bring a degree of happiness into the lives of those less blessed than we are. We walk away feeling righteous, believing we have fulfilled our duty as spiritual, religious, caring, human beings.

There is a tradition in Judaism called tzedakah, which, very loosely translated, means "charity." But, while charity involves decision, tzedakah does not—it is an obligation. Charity is giving to the unfortunate to offset their adversities. Tzedakah goes beyond giving something to tide people over; it attempts to get people to, once again, stand with dignity. Even the indigent, who are sustained by charity, are compelled to give tzedakah so the act of receiving does not leave them without dignity.

I grew up in a spiritual Jewish family where doing for others was not a once-a-year holiday occurrence. There wasn't a day my father didn't remind us to share our good fortune. He made it clear that sharing was not a choice, that we were required to help others as naturally as we were expected to draw our next breath.

I smile today because I now recognize we were not even remotely wealthy. My father was a farmer—a "gentleman farmer," as he humbly referred to himself—who worked hard and died at the age of forty-six, never to see the fruits of his labor. There were many weeks we couldn't afford meat, fish, or chicken. We lived on whatever the land produced, Kraft macaroni and cheese, and Campbell's vegetarian and vegetable soup. But my father said we were fortunate and that's what my brother and I believed.

It was not unusual for us to find a tattered vagrant sitting at our breakfast table. My father, who regularly preached to us about the dangers of hitchhiking, would pick up strangers—people who looked down and out—and bring them home. He'd give them a cot to sleep on in our basement. In the morning Mother would prepare them a large, hot breakfast and a bagged lunch. Then my father would slip them a five-dollar bill, a great deal of money for us back in the early fifties, and drive them to some reasonable destination.

When my brother grew up and moved to Manhattan, he regularly filled large shopping bags with peanut butter and jelly sandwiches, apples, oranges, and bananas, and walked the streets handing out food to the homeless.

As a teenager I traveled by bus to a neighboring town where I worked summers, without pay, in an orphanage.

In today's complex, dot-com world of two-paycheck families, high-interest credit card payments, endless carpooling, interminable supermarket lines, and time-consuming high-tech communication devices, we barely have time to do for ourselves, much less think about doing for others. But there is a simple way to teach our children that we are not solely self-involved. In many Jewish homes, you will find a tzedakah box, a kind of piggy bank. Family members place all their end-of-the-day loose change from their purses and pockets into this bank. When the bank is full, the contents are donated to a synagogue, a church, or a trusted charity for families or individuals in need of assistance. It's so easy to do and such an invaluable example to set for our children.

Maintaining the spirit of tzedakah throughout the entire year enriches the lives of impoverished recipients. It enhances and intensifies the quality of each contributor's life as well.

KEEP MOVING

'TSNOW PROBLEM

J anice and I met while on a weight loss program in North Carolina. No need for further explanation. At 7:30 each morning we dragged ourselves one mile to exercise class. We always arrived exhausted and optimistic that the walk had yielded at least a five-pound loss.

It never happened.

One morning we awoke to a foot of snow. In my home state of New Jersey snowfalls are routine, but in the South, schools close, shopkeepers lock up, and residents cower behind closed doors and pray they'll have enough food to carry them through the siege.

With its limited number of snowplows, the state was not equipped to handle snowfalls. So only a handful of courageous motorists chance driving the unplowed roads. Most end up crashing because they're unable to avert their gaze from the unfamiliar white stuff falling from the sky.

I looked at Janice.

"Did you bring boots?" I asked.

"To North Carolina? Get real. Let's take my car."

We wrapped plastic shopping bags over our Reeboks and trudged to the parking lot where we scraped ice and snow from car windows, got in, warmed up the engine, and thawed our hands.

Janice put the car into reverse. It wouldn't move. The wheels spun defiantly.

"This is not good," she said.

We sat staring at each other, trying to come up with a doable solution, when we heard a knock on the driver's side window. We saw the face of a nice-looking man, probably in his forties.

"You gals need help?"

Janice lowered her window.

"We sure do!"

"Put it in reverse," he instructed. "I'll go in front and try to rock 'er. Gentle, okay? Real gentle."

He pushed the front of the car with a slow, steady, pulsating motion. The wheels spun and melted the snow beneath them. After ten minutes of pushing and rocking, Janice was able to back the car onto the street. We waved thanks to our gallant hero.

Slight problem: the angle of the wheels had forced the car to back out of the parking lot onto the one-way street, in the wrong direction. The rear of the car pointed toward our destination, but the front looked straight ahead at oncoming traffic.

"Holy shit!" Janice said. "What should I do?"

She was paralyzed. I was terrified.

"Put it into reverse and accelerate!" I yelled.

"You've got to be kidding."

"Now!"

Janice looked in the rearview mirror and shifted into reverse.

"I hate driving backwards. I've always hated driving backwards. We're gonna die!"

Had traffic been moving at its normal speed of 50-plus mph instead of eight, we'd have been instant roadkill. As it was, we stood a better chance of getting a ticket.

"I can't believe we're doing this," Janice whined. "We're crazy."

We looked at each other, giggled, and acknowledged our insanity.

As we continued going backwards, a Toyota moved closer to our front bumper. Our restrained giggles accelerated into full-blown hilarity.

Janice kept driving, looking over her right shoulder.

"Omigod! A red light!" she screamed. "I have to stop."

The Toyota, which was all but attached to our front bumper, also stopped. We stared into the face of a stiff, strait-laced man whose furrowed brow clearly displayed his disapproval of our caper. One look at him was all we needed to throw us into uncontrollable, sidesplitting hysterics.

With tears streaming down my face and hands pressed hard between my legs, I managed to spit out the words, "Get me back to the motel. Now! I just wet my pants."

That was all Janice needed to hear. She was laughing so hard, she could barely drive.

"I'm not turning around. Not even for you," she said. "When we get there, jump out, roll in the snow, and wet your whole body. Do that and nobody will notice your pants."

I did as she instructed.

The following day we shopped for boots.

And I bought new pants.

ABBY AT THE AIRPORT

M y daughter and I were in a small airport waiting for a connection to Saint Lucia. Abby looked at an assortment of rings in a small duty-free jewelry shop and couldn't decide which to buy.

After a while I said, "Abby, we have to go. The plane will be taking off soon."

Just then a pilot walked up alongside us.

"Don't worry," he said. "That plane isn't going anywhere without me."

He attempted to help my attractive daughter with her jewelry selection. After roughly five minutes, he looked at his watch and said, "You're on your own. I have to get to the plane."

Still indecisive, Abby frantically waved her arms and squealed, "Which one? Which one?"

The pilot looked back over his shoulder, pointed and shouted, "That large silver-gray one with big wings."

ADVENTURES iN MY SHiNY RED CONVERTiBLE

I rolled my cart out of the supermarket and filled my trunk with bags of groceries. There was no room for the twelve-pack of toilet tissue so I placed it in the back seat. (I don't understand why toilet "tissue" is an acceptable, gentler phrase than toilet "paper" when it's the word "toilet," and not "paper," that should be softened.) My allergies had been acting up, so I poked a hole in the outer plastic wrap of one roll and ripped off several squares in preparation for my next sneeze.

I was in my brand new red Chrysler Sebring convertible. Perfect temperatures prompted me to put my top down. Not mine, actually, my car's.

Balmy breezes blew my recent bleach job into frenzied circles as I drove north on Route 206. I felt everyone's eyes on me. I'd waited a lifetime for that convertible. Usually pragmatic, I'd always pushed aside fanciful, impractical dreams and written them off as silly, extravagant, or unnecessary. After all, one has to be nuts to own a convertible in New Jersey where winter weather conditions could wreak havoc on the canvas top and certainly would limit the days I could actually drive with the top down. But I'd had a landmark birthday and, with a little encouragement from the man in my life, I threw caution to the wind and bought it.

So there I was, feeling absolutely wonderful, enjoying the smiles and waves of passing drivers and pedestrians, when from the corner of my eye I saw something white—and it was fluttering. I turned my head to see the better part of a roll of toilet paper flying in the wind behind me.

I was mortified and deflated when I realized neither my new blonde hair nor my classy red car was the reason for all the attention.

I headed home on Route 80, at roughly 68 mph, surrounded on all sides by cars moving at the same pace. Suddenly an enormous black tire came rolling toward me at warp speed. There wasn't a thing I could do to avoid it. I was surrounded on both sides by moving vehicles, but this tire only wanted me. Before I could blink—bang!—it had smashed into my front right bumper and flown over the top of my car, never to be seen again.

I heard metal drop onto the highway. My gaze darted in all directions to see if I could spot a disabled vehicle throwing off sparks as it scraped along the macadam. But I saw nothing more than the relieved, grateful faces of surrounding drivers as I limped my way first to the right lane, then to the shoulder. I jumped out of the car and surveyed the damage.

My hood was badly dented, and there were black tread marks where the tire had hit and bounced off. They were wide and huge and had to be from an 18-wheeler. My bumper was destroyed. My right headlight was dangling just inches from the ground.

I whipped out my cell phone, the one I'd bought specifically for times like this—and tried to call the state police. There was no signal. So I tucked my headlight back into its hole and drove the remaining thirty miles home, filled with trepidation, waiting for additional parts to drop onto the road or for the car to explode, or implode, or do whatever it is cars do when forced to drive in such conditions.

I made it home.

The next day I brought it to Bob at my friendly car repair shop. He was waiting on someone. When I walked in, he looked up, smiled broadly, and introduced me.

"Laverne is one of my best customers," he said, which didn't please me at all.

When I picked up my car several days later and walked out, I turned back and said, "I never want to see you again!!"

"No hard feelings," he laughed.

We agreed this would be our last exchange.

As it happened, one of us was lying.

I NEED MY OWN LANDiNG STRiP

We vacationed in Savannah, Georgia with my son and his wife, and spent time with our grandson Max, a budding fashion photographer, at Savannah College of Art and Design (SCAD).

Savannah has many tourist attractions: the Savannah River, River Street's quaint shops, excellent restaurants, gargantuan trees with widespread branches and hanging moss that sway in gentle breezes. Mostly, I enjoyed the immense candy shops that specialize in everything pecan.

I can walk short distances, but in time my back rebels, so it's easier for everyone if I display a level of independence in my motorized scooter. I admit to running over toes and backing into Achilles' heels and brick structures that materialize from nowhere just to embarrass me. My greatest challenges are curbs that pretend to be friendly, then suddenly slant or split, out of spite, which is exactly what happened. Just as I prepared to roll over a curb, it pulled a Red Sea, causing me to tilt to the right, land on my right elbow, hip and knee, and bleed on my daughter-in-law's brand new white shirt.

One day we drove an hour and a half to Driftwood Beach on Jekyll Island, where we watched Max direct a photo shoot with his team of three female students. The landscape was jaw-dropping—full-grown gigantic driftwood trees lying on their sides and acres of massive rocks and cement chunks that only the surefooted would attempt to navigate. It looked like Mother

Nature had once played havoc in the form of a hurricane or tornado. For this adventure my walker assisted me over the hard, damp sand. I accepted help navigating the softer, deeper sand.

We left the beach later than planned, so rather than return to our hotel to shower and dress before dinner, my daughter-in-law suggested she and I change in the car. I wasn't sure that I, an octogenarian, could make the rapid, fluid moves required to remove my one-piece swimsuit, hook my bra, and slip into my panties, slacks, and shirt, and still maintain a semblance of dignity. I knew that if I wasn't up to the task, my poor daughter-in-law would see things she would never be able to unsee. But in the interest of good sportsmanship, I decided to go for it.

Andrea hung a large beach towel between the headrests of the two front seats, where the men sat, while we searched various bags for our clothing, which wound up strewn over the back seat and floor. I located my black-and-white-flecked slacks, but my white shirt and black undies were nowhere to be found.

We both doubled over in convulsive laughter as Andrea ripped off her brown T-shirt.

"Here," she directed. "Wear this."

It's important to note that Andrea is roughly four sizes smaller than I am. I've no doubt that the sight of me in her itty-bitty brown shirt and my black-and-white-flecked slacks could be used by doctors to induce vomiting.

Andrea was left with no option but to wear her fleece-lined gray hoodie. The temperature was 86 humid degrees. When I looked closely I saw her melting.

In a nick of time my white shirt turned up, but our frantic search for my undies was futile. Worse than the thought of not finding them was the thought that someone else would. I had no choice but to go commando, which was surprisingly breezy and pleasant.

The following day we went to a terrific all-you-can-eat-for-$20 sushi restaurant. I was using my walker. At the end of the meal, while we waited for Mighty Marc to join us outdoors, I sat on my walker's seat, and as though on cue, a wheel buckled. Once again, I tumbled onto the cement. This time my injuries were more serious. I landed on my left hip, thigh, and shoulder, in pain—not the kind that signaled something was broken, just seriously bruised.

It was then we remembered that wheel had been broken on another vacation, and that walker should have been thrown out.

Since I'm on a blood thinner, I knew the massive area of intense black and blue would not disappear in time for swimsuit weather. But if I dare to put on a bathing suit, it's comforting to know that all eyes will be on my purple thigh, and no one will notice my cellulite or the scars from my one hip replacement or two knee replacements

I make a point to always carry a flashlight for those times I'm unable to see the bright side.

JUST ANOTHER DAY iN HELL

I was lying on my back, arms raised over my head, getting radiation for breast cancer. Blinking was the only movement allowed. While radiation was a breeze, within five minutes of lying in that position my shoulders felt like they were resting on knives.

It was my first radiation session. Afterwards I met with a cancer center representative whose job was to point out the many support tools available to me and watch over my well-being.

"Have you been under any stress lately?" she asked.

"Yes," I answered. "As a matter of fact, I have."

With sincere concern on her face, she leaned in to me.

"Tell me what's bothering you."

"I have cancer."

She paused and smiled weakly. I knew she genuinely wanted to help but, given the circumstances, I thought the question was bizarre.

"Besides that?" she asked.

"Besides cancer? Hmm. My radiation schedule conflicts with my hair and nail appointments."

If she appreciated my humor, she didn't let on.

"We offer a number of support groups you might find beneficial," she said.

"I can see where they might be helpful to many people, but I've never been a joiner," I replied. "In fact, I'm looking for a way out of this Breast Cancer Club."

She handed me three pounds of brochures, leaflets, and questionnaires.

Next I met with a nutritionist who explained the importance of eating vegetables and keeping my weight down. My kind of cancer feeds off estrogen, which is stored in fat, she explained. Then she said that, basically, if I find myself enjoying what I'm eating, I'm not eating properly.

I explained that I have had countess decades to form friendships with vegetables, but it hadn't happened.

"While it's difficult to believe that it's ever going to happen," I said, "I understand the importance of at least inviting them to dinner." I promised I would.

My sessions with the two support staff members took longer than I'd anticipated. I found myself rushing to the dermatologist, where I was scheduled to have a wart removed from the top of my foot.

By the time the wart was removed, it was three o'clock, and I still hadn't eaten breakfast, or gone to the market, as I'd planned.

I pulled up to the window at McDonald's—a place I frequent about three times a year—and spoke to the garbled voice behind the food selection sign.

"What's better?" I asked. "The grilled chicken or the fried fish?"

"I don't like fish," she said, "but the grilled chicken is delicious."

"I was hoping you'd say that. I shouldn't eat anything fried, so chicken it is."

"That will be $1.70," she said. "Go to Window One."

I pulled up to Window One and gave her one dollar and three quarters.

She handed me a penny.

"I'm sorry," I said, smiling, "but this isn't correct."

"Really? What was I supposed to give you?"

"Five cents."

"Oh."

She took the penny from my hand and gave me a nickel. I wondered how much she pocketed each day. I drove to Window Two, retrieved my food, pulled into a parking space, opened my bag, and found a deep-fried fish sandwich in a brown wrapper that read "Chicken."

I decided that since I hadn't ordered it, the calories wouldn't count.

McDonald's shares a parking lot with the market, so I exited my car and walked toward shopping carts, which were neatly lined up roughly three miles from the entrance. A young man approached.

"Are you alright, ma'am?" he asked.

"Yes, I'm fine. Why?"

He pointed to my foot. I was stunned. The top of my foot, my shoe, and the hem of my jeans were covered with blood. I'd forgotten to tell my dermatologist that I'm on a blood thinner, which causes me to bleed more heavily than I normally would.

"Do you want me to get help?"

"No. I'll be fine, but I would appreciate it if you get me a cart," I said. "I'll go inside, grab Band-Aids, and clean up."

I found the Band-Aids and headed for the bathroom, leaving a narrow trail of blood. I have no way of knowing who noticed, but if that young man saw my trail on a macadam parking lot, I suspect marketers noticed it on the blonde wooden floor.

While at the market, I decided to get a flu shot. I filled out the paperwork, mentioned I was getting radiation, and was told I needed approval from my oncologist. Three phone calls later, I received approval.

Radiation commonly leaves patients tired and I was, at that point, exhausted. Yet, somehow, I survived the day and could even see humor in it.

Driving home, I remembered something that happened in seventh or eighth grade. The health class teacher told the girls that if we were able to hold a pencil under our breast without dropping it, it was time to wear a bra.

I raised my hand.

"I think I waited too long," I said. "I'm able to hold the entire pencil box."

I should have realized back then my girls would, one day, lead me to trouble.

THERE'S NO PLACE LiKE IT

We decided to do something different—different for us. We always take vacations out of the country. During the weeks before leaving, we whine a lot. By we, I mean me. I've never gotten the knack of packing and always return with a suitcase full of clothes I never wore.

Shuttle costs to and from the airport are exorbitant. Then there's the agony of airport lines, getting through security, physical discomfort on planes, and inedible airplane food. On our last trip I ordered a fruit and cheese platter. The photograph on the menu had me drooling. What I got—I kid you not—were three one-inch cheese squares, three crackers, and, I swear, two tiny dried apricot slices, for $7.98.

Because I've had so many joint replacements, Security has to pat me down, always assigning unattractive women to the task instead of the handsome men I request.

During my last pat down, I stood in a small glass booth, hands out at my sides, legs spread, when Mighty Marc, who stood just outside the booth, decided he needed his passport. Since I was carrying it, he reached for the doorknob and came this close to being shot when armed guards grabbed and frisked him. It happened so fast, neither of us knew what the hell was happening.

So the next time I said, "Let's take a road trip. We have friends and relatives up and down the East Coast. Wouldn't it be fun to spend several days with each of them and visit landmarks along the way?"

He gave me thumbs up.

AAA helped plan the route. What fun we would have!

"Let's make it a real adventure and rent a mobile home," Marc said. "Why pay for motels and spend money eating every meal out? Instead, you can prepare meals while I drive."

"Sweetheart," I said, "do you remember our beautiful, renovated kitchen with every modern convenience? If so, then you must certainly know I've never been in it. So why would I enjoy cooking on vacation in a small box on wheels?"

We looked at a mobile home that was described as spacious. By spacious, they meant large enough to comfortably accommodate three generations of mice. It had a lovely wood interior and a literally wall-to-wall king-size bed that could only be accessed from the foot of the bed.

Packing would be easy. Each of the two silverware drawers would comfortably hold two shirts. There was space for two-and-a-half pairs of shoes in the cabinet over the fridge, and ample room for toiletries and cosmetics in the oven I had no plans to use.

I had some trouble getting through the narrow bathroom door but was assured that, after a week or so, I'd get the hang of sliding in sideways.

We were advised to park at campsites and take taxis to our destinations. I let that thought marinate for about forty-five seconds. Then I said, "Honey, maybe a plane trip wouldn't be so bad, after all. Flying domestic is easier than overseas. We could rent a car at the airport and drive to each destination."

"Makes sense," Marc said.

We began investigating plane schedules and fares.

Three days later, I said, "Do you remember that fun train trip we took to Florida several years back? We even brought our car with us. Maybe we should consider doing that this time. As I recall, the train restaurant was excellent."

"Good idea, if that's what you want," he said. "I'll check into it."

We were excited, so I notified everyone and informed them when to expect us.

A week went by.

"Remind me," I said, nervously. "Why do we want a vacation that requires endless hours of driving, hanging out at people's homes, using their washing machines, then driving a whole lot more?"

"We wanted to visit our grandson in Savannah during his first year in college," he said. "Why? Are you having fifth thoughts?"

"Well," I said, "let's just say that nothing about this trip is exciting me."

He smiled.

"Here's a thought. Let's stay home," he said. "We love our home. Why would we want to be anywhere else this time of year?"

"I know. My feelings exactly. We can plan several weekend getaways."

"Now that's a plan I can live with," he said.

"I'm so relieved. This is the happiest I've been since we decided to take a vacation."

"I'm thinking our next vacation should be restful," he said. "We should lounge around and barely do anything but read, and we should have all our meals served to us."

"Like a prison cell?"

"Exactly."

OH, NO, NOT AGAIN!

We were driving home from Connecticut to New Jersey after a lovely weekend with our son and his family. We'd made the trip countless times. It's an easy ride with no major turns: I-95 to I-287 to I-80.

Around an hour from home, I turned to Mighty Marc.

"I don't remember seeing those buildings before, do you?" I asked.

He squinted at the landscape.

"No. They weren't here last trip. How could they have built an entire shopping and apartment complex in just three weeks?"

"And look over there." I pointed. "They've also built a river."

"Yeah, I can see that. Where the hell are we?"

"It's hard to tell. All the road signs are in French."

Something was very wrong. We recognized nothing. It was apparent we'd veered off the main highway. That's virtually impossible to do, but somehow we'd managed it.

We discussed how and where it had happened as we drove through a new town—new to us, that is. So it shouldn't be a total loss, we stopped for a bite to eat and asked for directions to the Tappan Zee Bridge.

It wasn't the first time something like that had occurred. We've bypassed destinations we know as well as the rooms in our house, sometimes driving as much as twelve to fifteen miles before realizing we missed our mark.

There's a reason this happens. It has nothing to do with senility and everything to do with our inability to shut up. We become so immersed in conversation that we completely forget we're in a car, heading for a destination. It's happened often enough that nearly every time we enter a car, one of us tries to remember to remind the other one that this time we're going to pay attention.

It rarely happens.

Our jabbering can be about politics, religion, family, fashion, or tattoos. Like the time we drove past a herd of cows, in a field, standing in a circle, with each cow facing into the center.

"Look," I said, "they're having a cowwow."

We laughed.

And got lost.

One time we were heading for a specific restaurant, around forty minutes from the house. I had been to the doctor that afternoon for a routine checkup, as if checkups at my age are ever routine. While Mighty Marc drove, I reported the details of my visit.

"The doctor said I'm in good health, so I reminded him that ten years earlier he had said I needn't be concerned about my heart murmur for at least ten years. I told him I'm starting to worry. So he changed my deadline. Now I don't have to worry for another twenty years."

"Seriously?" Marc said. "I don't want to upset you, but odds are you won't be here in twenty years."

"Exactly."

"But just in case I am here, as I was leaving the doctor's office, I started talking to an elderly woman who was with her husband. She told me that three years earlier the doctor said she, too, had another twenty years, but she recently decided she no longer wanted them all. I asked if I could have some of hers. She looked to her husband for approval. He nodded, and they agreed to give me six. Isn't that terrific?"

We discussed the ramifications of living that long: which of us could be trusted to cook without burning down the house, who would run over the most people on the road, what color motorized scooter we each wanted, and how many thousands of times each of us would say "What?" to the other. Before we knew it, we were driving through what I'm pretty sure was Canada.

I love having a man who enjoys conversing with me—someone who actually listens and gives me feedback. But not now, not with the price of gas so high.

DOCTOR'S REPORT

My pain management doctor thought I might need a hip replacement and sent me to get an X-ray. I told him my last doctor had ordered a hip X-ray two months earlier, and my hip was fine. Unconvinced, he asked me to bring him that X-ray and the accompanying report.

I found both and decided to read the report. In the middle of all the medical jargon, was the line: "The patient was well groomed."

How my grooming was even remotely relevant to my medical condition, I couldn't imagine. Yet in some strange way, it pleased me to know I'd passed his high standards.

When I returned to my pain management doctor, I handed everything over to him.

"I was happy to read that my report includes the fact the doctor thought I was well groomed," I gloated.

My bubble burst when he said, "These reports only allow us to select one of two choices. The other is 'disheveled.'"

GULLiBLE'S TRAVELS

y cataracts were removed several years ago. So when my sight once again became foggy, I thought the darn things had either grown back or I was going blind. My ophthalmologist quelled my fears when he said that cataracts do not grow back but, in 20 percent of cases, lenses become cloudy.

A three-minute laser treatment repaired the problem but left me with the same terrible side effects as when my cataracts were removed: deep wrinkles and liver spots appeared on my face. My husband insists they were there before the laser treatment. He's wrong. If I knew I looked like this before, I would never have opted for clearer vision.

I was whining about this appalling side effect to a friend, who recommended the Miracle Pill she had seen on the Dr. Oz Show, guaranteed to diminish the appearance of fine lines and wrinkles in six weeks. Six weeks, at my age, is a long time to wait, but I wasn't going anywhere looking like I did. Worst-case scenario, I thought, I'll look good at my funeral. I ordered it.

Shortly thereafter I was drawn in again while watching the TV show, *The Doctors*, which consists of a panel of doctors who discuss health issues. The lead doctor is Travis Stork.

A product called Wrinkle Butter was being touted as the latest breakthrough in skin care. They said it had countless anti-aging benefits. A woman in a white lab coat smeared Wrinkle

Butter over Dr. Stork's face. Her white lab coat assured me she was an authority.

I became leery when I learned the product being rubbed over the doctor's face came "from the bowels of earthworms." They called it "worm castings" and said Wrinkle Butter was filled with peptides and enzymes clinically proven to repair damaged skin. I had no idea what a peptide was. But I did know that anything from the bowels of earthworms is worm poop.

I wondered how scientists came up with the idea of smearing it over a woman's face. Was the decision unanimous? Was it first tested on wrinkled rats? Had they even considered using it for anything else first? Like fuel? Or shoe polish?

But I was blinded by the promise of dewy skin, so I ordered a jar for myself and another for my daughter. What loving mother doesn't want her daughter to experience the pleasure of smearing worm poop over her face?

When the package arrived, I opened the jar and stared in disbelief. I don't know what the hell they smeared on Dr. Stork's face, but it most definitely was not the same product that arrived in my mailbox. While his face had been covered with a white cream, my jar was filled with brown stuff—brown enough to remind me of what it actually was.

I stared at it for several days, garnering the courage to use it. On the fourth day I gingerly dabbed it on my face. I tried to ignore the small particles of grit that were probably obtained from right under the worm during the poop scoop. I suspected that rather than spend time and money refining the product, they opted to leave it in, hoping women would accept it as an exfoliant.

After two weeks of nightly applications, my wrinkles still glared at me. Since I was having difficulty getting past the product's color, I was only too happy to drop-kick it into the trash, as did my daughter.

Dr. Oz's Miracle Pill finally arrived. I carefully read the directions and conscientiously took a pill every single day for the recommended six weeks. And, while I swallowed the Miracle Pills and waited patiently for the "appearance of fine lines and wrinkles" to diminish, I saw yet another of Dr. Oz's shows. That time he recommended an all-natural-ingredients diet pill.

I still had faith in Dr. Oz. After all, Oprah had endorsed him so I knew he was the real deal. If he said my face would, once again, be wrinkle free, I knew it would.

It never happened.

But since I'm always looking for a quick and easy diet fix, I ordered three bottles of his all-natural-ingredients diet pills. Directions said to take one pill twice daily, and I could lose between seven and ten pounds the first week. I was psyched and began shopping for a new wardrobe. I even gave a bottle to my son.

After a week and a half, my son lost ten pounds. I gained three.

There's a Cherokee Indian at my door selling an elixir he promises will get rid of my arthritis, cellulite, and toenail fungus. I'm a little skeptical but he has a website, so he must be legitimate. I mean, everyone knows that if you read it on the Internet, it's true. Right?

I'm told there's a fine line between naiveté and stupidity. It scares me to think that somewhere along the way I may have stepped over it.

IN THE POOL WITH OLD PEOPLE

My thirties and forties brought a slew of ailments and bodily assaults that left my once lovely torso looking like a map of the Manhattan subway system. My exterior still looked good, though, and I had energy.

God, I miss energy.

It wasn't until my early sixties that I noticed obvious signs of wear and tear on my body. I was losing my battle with gravity, which was pulling me closer to my feet.

While I'd been focusing on gray hairs and wrinkles, my right foot had developed a large red bunion and a hammertoe, signaling the end of sexy sandals. This realization was more devastating than my belly scars. I have worshiped shoes my entire life. My closet overflows with them.

I envisioned a future of frumpy flats and laced orthotics— almost too painful to think about.

Along with severe back arthritis, replacements of one hip and two knees had me leaning on a cane and, occasionally, a walker. When I passed a mirror, I was shocked to see my posture resembled that of Quasimodo. Like a periscope in search of land, my head stretched two feet in front of me when I walked. Hopes of making it with George Clooney had long since vanished.

Gravity also had worked overtime on my once perky boobs. I could tuck them into the elastic waistband of my sweatpants, which managed them far more effectively than a sports bra. And, saddest of all, my face had begun to look like a Shar-Pei's.

All this in mind, I was with my husband at a lovely Florida resort. He sat under a beach umbrella, sketching, while I made my way to the pool. Even though I hated the body I used to be proud of in a swimsuit, I could not give up romping in the water.

I clung to the hot metal rail until I reached the bottom step into the pool, then made my way toward an animated group of my peers. I walked on my toenails, trying to avoid the cold water as long as possible. Every few steps I stopped to splash water on my chest the way my mother had done, and I swore I never would.

The five strangers in the pool were old, wrinkled, and for the most part, overweight with varicose veins, liver spots, wrinkled chests, floppy upper arms, and cellulite thighs. They all looked like me. The men had nose and ear hairs. Actually, several women did, too.

Being timeworn granted me automatic membership into this group of strangers.

I worked my way to the edge of the circle, where they warmly welcomed me. Before I could say "Lipitor," the conversation was flowing. I learned more than I ever wanted to know about stents, enlarged prostates, angina, osteoporosis, dementia, atrial fibrillation, arthritis, hip and knee replacements, back pain, epidurals, and—God help me—incontinence.

When we finally disbanded I was surprised to realize the spirit in this group had uplifted me. Most were suffering from one ailment or another but they all were determined to enjoy this period of their lives. They were doing things they'd promised themselves they'd do when the children were grown. When they'd saved enough money. When they retired. They were traveling, painting, writing, learning to play guitar, teaching, moving to the city, going back to school, and living myriad dreams and yearnings put on hold their whole lives.

My parents' generation didn't have the benefit of modern medicine and technology. We're living considerably longer than they did. My father died of heart complications at age forty-six—something far less apt to happen today. Because he died so young, I am able to remember him strong, handsome, and always working. Because I've been fortunate to live far longer than my father, my children are not going to remember me young, strong, and pretty. But they will remember me old, actively involved, and happy.

Surgeries, wrinkles, aches, pains, and low energy are tolls we all pay for the privilege of longevity. Fortunately, spunk, zest, and tenacity are free.

TECHNOLOGY GIVES ME A HEADACHE

I didn't want a cell phone. I was perfectly content with my landline and felt no need to reach out, touch, or be touched by anyone. I loved the quiet periods that came with driving and wandering through shops and parks, alone and noncommunicative. Now if I don't answer my phone in the middle of dinner at a restaurant, callers worry and later reprimand me for having turned it off.

Technology frustrates and baffles me. When I reluctantly caved in and bought a cell phone, I did it so I could call for help if I was lost or mugged. I hadn't bargained for a built-in camera, a recording device, access to the Internet, e-mail and texting capabilities, games, a calculator, and dozens of other alleged amenities that I never use, don't need, and don't understand. I resent being prompted by a robot who doesn't react when I scream obscenities at it. My greatest technological accomplishment this year was learning how to turn up my cell phone's volume.

I watched a twelve-year-old text messaging on his cell phone. His fingers raced over the keypad nearly as fast as Kim Kardashian's ass expanded. I thought, If he can do it, I can, too, but he'd typed and sent a ten-word message while I searched for the "i" in "Hi."

My teenage granddaughter sent me an e-mail from her cell phone during History class in school. As if that wasn't bad enough, she used text messaging abbreviations. She might as well have typed it in Swahili. To make a point, I responded using a form of shorthand I'd learned in an adult education course. She answered saying she hadn't understood a word, which made me feel good.

Computers drive me crazy, too. I miss my Underwood typewriter. The only time I worried about it crashing was when it sat too close to the edge of my desk. I could type obscene letters and bomb threats and not worry about incriminating evidence being stored in its innards. It never caught a virus or sent me messages on how to enlarge my manhood.

I do admit, though, that the Internet is wonderful for research. As a full-blown dyslexic, it's far easier for me to navigate the Net than use the Dewey Decimal System at the library, where my repeated number reversals always had me searching for books in the wrong section.

Before I learned how to use the World Wide Web, I didn't know I needed the six-foot-long bronze sculpture now in my front yard. I didn't realize my home could be enhanced if I bought that twenty-inch-high silver end table that I may have to hang from the ceiling because I have no space on the floor. I didn't realize the ease of ordering all kinds of makeup, miracle diet pills, miracle wrinkle creams, books, shoes, and exotic foods. I never enjoyed the friendship of so many hundreds of people I probably wouldn't like if I ever actually met and knew them.

Before the Internet my credit card statements were white with small areas of black as opposed to this month's statement, which is black with tiny patches of white.

My husband surprised me with a TiVo television recorder for my birthday. It was a lovely gesture, but he failed to take into account that it had taken me four months to understand my old VCR and three weeks to figure out how to set my digital alarm clock. After six years I still don't know how to program my convection oven.

I admit I enjoy my digital camera, which has the ability to hold several hundred photos. It's wonderful being able to snap pictures and instantly look at the camera's small screen to view images of places I've been, family gatherings, and memorable celebrations. But I've now taken several hundred pictures and have no more room to take more. I don't know how to get them out of my camera, into my computer, onto my screen, and printed. I suspect it's time to buy an additional digital camera.

Before computers, cell phones, digital cameras, and TiVo recorders, I actually thought I was smart. Not the case anymore. I now agree with my granddaughter, who calls me Techno-Amish.

THE SEXES

SAY WHAT?

S ince we're both retired Mighty Marc and I generally go marketing together. I make two shopping lists—one for my side of the market, one for his.

One day his list had him picking up my medication at the pharmacy. When we met at the cash register, I asked, "Did you get my pills?"

"Yes," he said. "That prescription cost $141. I couldn't believe it."

"I know," I said. "I pay that every month."

"Are you sure the prescription wasn't for birth control pills?" he asked.

"Are you crazy? I'm seventy-eight years old. My ovaries have dried, died, and gone to ovary heaven. Why would I need birth control pills?"

"For that kind of money, for sure you're getting screwed."

UNSUPPORTED EVIDENCE

Are women better off not wearing bras? This topic on nighttime news, squeezed between Korea's nuclear threats and the start of baseball season, has women voicing strong opinions. I, of course, am one of those women. My first reaction is a resounding, "OMG! YES! YES! YES!"

Jean-Denis Rouillon, a professor at the University of Franche-Comté in Besancon, France, conducted a study in which he examined the breasts of three hundred women, aged eighteen through thirty-five, over a fifteen-year period. His study concluded two things: "Bras provide no benefit to women and may actually be harmful to breasts over time" and "Medically, physiologically, and anatomically, the breast does not benefit from being deprived of gravity."

I must step in here and applaud Professor Rouillon for his courage in taking on such an arduous assignment. This brave man single-handedly (okay, maybe he used both hands) examined the breasts of three hundred young women over a fifteen-year period. He worked long, hard hours.

"Hi, honey. Don't hold dinner for me. I'll be working late. Yes, again."

Capucine Vercellotti, a twenty-eight-year-old woman who participated in the research, found that she breathed easier without the constraints of a bra. No kidding, Capucine. The only place I fully enjoy breathing is in the shower.

I knew from the first day I forced my arms behind my back and blindly attempted to find teensy metal hooks to fit into weensy metal eyes that constraining and compressing my breasts was not in my best interest. Like caged animals, my girls have always cursed the inhuman individual who saw the need to restrain this part of my anatomy. All they ever wanted was to be free.

Maybe it made a modicum of sense to cover them in 1914 when nineteen-year-old Mary Phelps Jacob tied a couple of silk handkerchiefs together to conceal stiff whalebone stays visible through her sheer gown. But before long the notion became a popular fashion statement as style-conscious women saw another way to start and follow a trend.

As luck would have it, someone, somewhere, decided those little silk handkerchiefs should do more than conceal whalebone. They might as well also lift and support because—heaven forbid—time and gravity would eventually have their way and breasts would lose the youthful perkiness God, and most men, believe they should have.

I love being a woman. I have never wanted to be a man, but when it comes to fashion, sometimes women are morons. I say this knowing full well I'll be slammed by most of the female population. The greater majority will rush out and buy anything that fashion magazines dictate. If they'd clearly thought through this bra issue nearly one hundred years ago, though, millions of women would not have dents in their shoulders from carrying around the weight of the world, and their midriffs would not have to tolerate irritating fabric rub. And for what? Just so bosoms won't bounce?

Seriously?

I've harnessed my girls every day of my life since eighth grade. When I told my mother that Jackie Young had winked and asked what I had in my gym suit pocket, she said it was time for me to wear a bra. She promised that if I always wore it, my breasts would never sag. Despite more than six painful decades of doing what Mother said, I have two words to describe what my girls look like today: National Geographic.

When I was in fourth grade I visited an eye doctor who prescribed glasses.

"Don't wear them all the time," he said, "or you will become too dependent on them."

I did what he suggested. I only wore them for seeing the blackboard, reading, and movies. Of course, the rest of the time I bumped into walls and got into strangers' cars. But the point is, I never found the need to rely on them. And so it should be with bras.

Rouillon cautioned that women who have worn bras for several decades would not benefit from taking them off now.

Wanna bet? Stand back.

ARE YOU FOR REAL?

When I moved from New Jersey to North Carolina in the early 1980s, I had just separated from my husband. I was there several weeks when I had trouble with what I thought might be a sty, under my right eyelid, so I made an appointment with an ophthalmologist. When I entered the office complex, I found myself in a large, crowded waiting room shared by clients of several adjoining offices.

When I finally got in to see Dr. Jones, as I'll call him, he informed me I had more than a sty. It was a sebaceous cyst that couldn't be dissolved with heat applications, as I'd hoped. The cyst would have to be cut, which frightened me. He gave me ointment and told me to go home, apply it to my lid, and report back in two days when he would lance it.

I had only been living in Durham a few weeks and didn't feel comfortable asking any of my new friends to drive me to and from the doctor, so when I returned to his office two days later, I took a cab. I was pretty sure I wouldn't be in shape to drive home after he sliced into my eyelid. The cab cost me twenty-four dollars one way, an enormous expense for me at that time in my life. I was newly separated and supporting myself as a temp with Kelly Girls until I found a permanent position.

The second time Dr. Jones examined my eye, he said it had improved and no longer needed lancing. I breathed a huge sigh of relief. I turned to leave.

"Would you allow me to drive you home?" he asked. "We can stop for cocktails on the way."

I was shocked.

"Don't you have patients waiting to see you?" I asked, pointing to a full waiting room.

"They can either reschedule or wait," he said.

All through my life my intuition had guided me. It never failed to direct me onto the right path. My gut told me Dr. Jones was not a nice man, and I would be a fool to let him drive me anywhere. I weighed the consequences of being trapped in a car with an unscrupulous ophthalmologist or taking another twenty-four dollar cab ride and not having lunch money for the next two weeks.

I hopped into his car. While it was apparent the man had no ethics, it was beyond question I had no brains.

I made it clear, up front, that I was not interested in cocktails. He wasn't shy about showing his disappointment as I directed him to my apartment. He persisted in asking me to have a drink—just one. I was nervous but equally adamant in saying no.

"I'm not comfortable with what might be misconstrued as unprofessional behavior," I said.

Might be? Ya' think?

When we arrived at my apartment I thanked him for his kindness, jumped out of his car, and all but flew up the walk to my door. Once in my apartment I thought about the risk I'd taken getting into his car and leading him directly to my door. All I could think was, Idiot!

Several weeks later I sat eating breakfast and reading the local daily newspaper when I saw the good doctor's photograph on the front page. It seemed my thoughtful, caring ophthalmologist had been carted off to jail for his involvement in a major fraud case. And that crowded waiting room was actually full of clients waiting to see hairdressers in the adjoining "office." For all I knew, Dr. Jones wasn't even an ophthalmologist, I never had a sebaceous cyst, and the ointment he gave me was a tube of hair gel.

I made a mental note to never again ignore my gut.

Do I REALLY WANT A MAN iN MY LiFE?

After a long hiatus from men, I returned to the dating scene. Online dating sounded wonderful, so I wrote a bio that painted a clear picture of who I am. I included that I wasn't interested in a committed relationship. Apparently, that appealed to most men. I was flooded with responses.

I learned that two weeks of daily correspondence with a person can offer more insight than a dozen traditional dates. Intellect, sense of humor, goals, tolerances, passions, politics, prejudices, and countless subtleties are rapidly revealed in and between the lines.

I discovered that time hadn't changed men's primal urges with one difference: finesse and patience were lacking. Men had the notion that divorcées should be grateful for attention bestowed upon them after long years of neglect by their husbands. Sadly, in many cases their assessment was accurate.

Lying, mostly regarding age and marital status, is rampant online. But the fact I trusted no one didn't ruin the fun I was having.

Good looks and chemistry matter to me, but chemistry is the sum total of a person, not merely an attractive face. Monty's photo was not particularly appealing to me, but our conversations were fascinating. He won me over with his sense of humor and intelligence. I doubt I would have given him a second glance had we not first experienced hours of riveting conversation that revealed his brilliant personality.

Henry worked in an abbey. I had no idea what he did there since he was intentionally secretive. I agreed to meet him out of curiosity and because he only lived eight miles away. His claim to fame was he fed squirrels without benefit of heavy, protective gloves.

He showed up in rumpled bib coveralls, a dingy under-shirt, and dirty work boots. He looked at me and said, "You're fatter than your picture." I resisted saying, "You're more re-volting than yours." He sprung for a Coke and a bag of Ruffles potato chips. It was the only time I went out with a man I met online and didn't offer to share the bill.

After months of delightful online conversation with Brent, I agreed to take the train to meet him. He had told me that he missed Jewish delis so I brought a huge box of, among other delicacies, corned beef, pastrami, chopped liver, and Jewish rye bread.

I entered his condo and found the dining room table beau-tifully set with fine china, silverware, and crystal goblets. I com-mented on how lovely it looked, and he said his table is always set. A closer look revealed half an inch of dust on everything. He wasn't lying.

There were two other oddities: When Brent shopped, he bought two of everything—from shirts to can openers to televi-sions—and his diet consisted solely of pizza, burgers, and cold cuts.

While Brent was very nice, he was a little too eccentric for me.

Then I met Marc. He had lived in San Diego for most of his forty-seven-year marriage. Recently, though, he'd moved to West Virginia to be with a daughter who'd offered to help him care for her mother, who suffered from Alzheimer's. Marc had been sole caretaker of his wife for ten years, during a time when support groups were nonexistent.

He was looking for marriage. I was not. I had come from a suffocating twenty-three-year marriage, and all I wanted was freedom, independence, and a date when and if the mood struck—once every few months, maybe. For me, a happy relationship would have the man in my life living a minimum of five miles from me. Possibly further.

We exchanged lengthy e-mails, which evolved into six-hour phone conversations during which he asked if I curse.

"Is this a trick question?" I asked.

"No."

I paused, not knowing the right answer.

"Sometimes 'Oh darn!' just doesn't do it," I confessed.

It turned out he wanted a woman who knew how to spice up a conversation.

He told me that while living in San Diego, he had performed Off Broadway. I explained that while San Diego certainly was off Broadway, it was too, too far off Broadway to be considered Off Broadway. He'd thought that anything not on Broadway was classified as Off Broadway.

He wanted to get together. I would have been happy to have the relationship continue as it was. I loved flirting over the phone but had no interest in ever meeting him . . . or anyone. He wore me down, though. We agreed to meet in Baltimore.

It was a four-hour drive. The traffic was horrendous. Driving through Washington, DC, was a nightmare, so I tried calling him from my cell phone to explain I'd be late, but my phone couldn't get a signal. I hyperventilated. I was driving 70 mph, in traffic, while repeatedly trying to connect. Stupid and dangerous, but I was already a half hour late and had at least another hour to go. When I finally arrived at the hotel, I was breathless and sweating. I grabbed my suitcase and toiletries bag from the car and dragged them into the hotel lobby.

I spotted him immediately at the far end of the lobby. He wore cowboy boots, fitted jeans, and a sports jacket. His hands were in his pockets, his head was cocked, and he smiled sheepishly. I half expected him to say, "Aw, shucks," and kick a pebble. He reminded me of Gary Cooper. My heart flip-flopped.

I dropped my suitcases in the middle of the lobby and raced toward him as I apologized for my tardiness.

We walked to the lounge, where he moved two armchairs so they faced each other. We sat talking and laughing for four-and-a-half hours. We learned that growing up, he lived seven miles from me, and I was dating boys from his high school while he was attending it. The hotel manager approached and asked if the suitcases in the middle of the lobby were mine.

I'd forgotten to check in.

That was in May 2003. We married in 2005 and haven't been apart since.

BREAKiNG NEWS: MEN AND WOMEN ARE DiFFERENT

M ichael G. Conner, clinical and medical psychologist, writes that men are built for physical confrontation and their skulls are usually thicker than women's. This, of course, comes as no surprise to women. But what I didn't know was men's skulls are thick because they are "attracted to reckless behavior," which explains their interest in slaying dragons, battling alligators, and any excuse for a slugfest.

Dr. Conner says that "women have four times as many brain cells as men. While men rely on their left brain to solve one problem, one step at a time, women can more easily access both sides of their brain and focus on more than one problem at a time."

And that often drives men to distraction.

Throughout centuries men have protected and provided for their families. In caveman days they gathered firewood, invented tools, killed wild animals, and spent excessive time butting heads with dinosaurs—a sport well suited for thick skulls. The little women stayed home, created murals on cave walls, sported rabbit skin originals, prepared tasty bison recipes, gave birth on dirt floors, and did their best to stay one step ahead of diaper-free toddlers.

In the 1800s men left their families for months and drove cattle across long dangerous trails through mountains and valleys in harsh weather. Women stayed behind with the children. Their only responsibilities were to scrounge for food and fight off wolves and Indians, all from the comfort of their homes.

In the early 1900s men did their best to cocoon women from the harsh realities of the world. They seemed to know, instinctively, that women were best suited for domestic work. But obstinate, unappreciative women bucked and defied men's good intentions and insisted on battling for equality.

Men are often guarded when meeting other men. They intuitively know how much is safe to divulge. They discuss generic topics such as sports, politics, and the hot chick at the end of the bar. They mention the worldwide cruise they're planning (even if they're not) and the new Benz they're thinking about buying (even though they're not).

A woman usually will jump right in and lead with her mouth. Within five minutes of meeting another woman, she'll offer the name and number of her plastic surgeon and her shrink. She'll reveal that her husband had an affair, her son has learning disabilities, and her teenage daughter is promiscuous. She'll delight in discussing anything and everything about sex.

Up until the late 1970s men's and women's roles were fairly well defined. Men grappled with difficult undertakings such as wars, unemployment, taxes, and finding affordable World Series tickets. Women dealt with daily menu selections, Kermit and Cookie Monster, diaper changes, and perfecting faux smiles that hid their true feelings.

Recent years show the line between male and female roles is becoming blurred. Men are taking a more active part in homemaking and child-rearing, and women are thriving in the business world.

I was thinking about a television commercial that Joe Namath, Jets football star, made back in 1973. He struck a seductive pose while sporting a pair of Hanes pantyhose. He made that commercial in the middle of the sexual revolution. I don't know how men felt about it, but women loved that this handsome, brawny quarterback had the courage to show his feminine, sensitive side.

In my fantasy Namath, who had a huge following, could have gotten better mileage out of his celebrity by encouraging men to include pantyhose in their own wardrobes. If he'd done that, maybe stereotypical male/female roles would have been obliterated by now. I suspect, though, that after enduring the constricted waistbands and suffocating discomfort of pantyhose, Namath opted to shirk an opportunity to advance the sexual revolution and instead returned to smashing bodies and banging heads with other football titans. Personally, I think he dropped the ball.

Hey, it's my fantasy and I'm stickin' to it.

CAMPING: NOT FOR SISSIES

A friend in California wrote to me extolling the delights of camping. She proudly described her ingenuity in preparing a dozen ice cream-filled cones, packing them with dry ice, and finding them frozen and intact several hours later when she arrived at her designated campsite and served them to her grandchildren. I admit to being impressed with her resourcefulness, but I'm also bewildered as to why she'd do such a thing when she easily could have been served ice cream in a bug-free, air-conditioned ice cream parlor.

I confess. I'm not into camping. What I love is the idea of camping. It certainly sounds heavenly to be outdoors under wide open skies, draw in all that wonderful fresh air, and listen to nature's sweet consort. But I've had to face the reality that I'm too much of a prima donna to accept everything that goes with those amenities—things like ruining my manicure while pitching a tent, trading in perfume for smelly bug spray, sleeping on cold hard ground, trudging half a mile to pee, and searching for an electrical outlet for my curling iron. None of these are on my list of Favorite Things To Do.

I did it once. I couldn't wait to go. En route to the campsite a bird flew into our car grill and remained there for the entire three-hour trip. I imagine he got tired of flying and wanted someone to drive him to his destination. Obviously, he hadn't thought the whole thing through because while he certainly got there, he arrived in a somewhat messy, compressed state.

And then it poured and poured and poured. I sympathized with what Noah must have contended with. There I was in a confined area with one wet foul-smelling dog, two tent leaks, three irritable tentmates, and an infinite number of elusive mosquitoes.

I wanted to sleep in a comfy nightgown, but my seasoned camper friends laughed hysterically at that idea and called me a wimp. They opted to sleep in sopping wet jeans and I, being totally intimidated, followed suit and was miserable.

Actually, I only thought I was miserable. Real misery didn't rear its ugly head until the wee hours of the night when I found myself wandering blindly through the frightening darkness, in a torrential storm, in search of some godforsaken Public Pee House.

The next morning our little makeshift chairs sank into four inches of mud as we attempted to burn wet kindling and create a flame hot enough to solidify egg whites and kill at least some of the trichinosis in our bacon.

I learned something about myself that weekend: I'm too old to put up with unnecessary inconveniences. My favorite sleepaway adventure must include four walls in a five-star hotel. I still love nature but I discovered it's best viewed from hotel and cruise ship balconies.

WHEN GOOD MEN GO BAD

W hen Mighty Marc signed on for a relationship with me, neither of us had any idea how often he would be called upon to face the worse part of "For better and for worse" and "In sickness and in health." We were only married a short while when a back problem that had mildly plagued me during our courtship, began to interfere with our lifestyle. The doctor diagnosed me as having BBB, medical jargon for Badly Beat-up Back.

The bad news was that I had painful arthritis, stenosis, herniated and bulging discs, and slight scoliosis. The good news was my family finally knew I was not a hypochondriac.

Then I tore my Achilles' heel, had respiratory problems, two bouts with sciatica, and two with diverticulosis. In January 2009 my right knee was replaced. Two years later, my left was replaced. Some time after that, I traded in my left hip.

Through all of this Mighty Marc never complained about his role as nursemaid. But I felt terrible. He had been caregiver to his former wife for nearly ten years before she succumbed to Alzheimer's. Surely, he had earned the right to an easy second time around.

Every time I'm out of commission he does laundry, washes floors, vacuums, polishes furniture, and prepares gourmet meals that frequently include printed menus with colorful scenes of foreign countries. He brings me hot tea, surprises me with chocolate, rubs my feet, kisses me, and tells me I'm beautiful.

One thing good about being part of a senior-aged couple is that my looks and his eyesight are fading at about the same speed. Therefore, he doesn't notice that since my return from the hospital, my unruly hair might best be described as "homeless chic." My gray roots are so long, I look like I'm wearing a yarmulke, and barrettes are holding back my untweezed brows.

Mighty Marc chauffeured me to physical therapy and post-surgical blood work five days a week. I hated keeping him from his creative interests, but he always says he's happy to be there for me.

I make a point of showing appreciation.

As it happens, I am not as nice as my husband. I used to be. Honest. But that changed when I discovered what a monstrous patient he is. When he's sick, his sweetness and goodness are replaced with irritability, impatience, whining, and a short temper. This normally angelic, selfless man wants instant relief and hates that he cannot control the speed of his recovery. He rejects every nice thing I attempt to do for him, so I've learned to avoid him. No foot rubs. No hot cups of coffee. No special meals. Instead, I cautiously slip my arm through his slightly opened door, toss in a slab of raw meat, then slam the door shut.

Friends tell me their husbands are also petulant brats when they're ill. Men believe their blister, their splinter, their paper cut, their hangnail, their cold, is far worse than anyone else has ever experienced.

Mighty Marc was driving 75 mph on the highway when he leaned toward me and pointed to his neck.

"What do you see there?"

I moved in closer and squinted.

"Nothing."

"It can't be nothing. Put on your glasses."

"I don't see anything."

"Look harder. I'm sure there's a sizable lump. And it's bleeding."

"Nope. Nothing's there."

"When we get home, I'll need Neosporin and a bandage."

"You're kidding, right?"

"Just because you can't see it doesn't mean it's not there."

My friend Patti says when her good-natured husband is sick, he goes from Hero to Zero in no time flat. I think the Jekyll/Hyde syndrome has to do with men's belief that they're supposed to be macho, and they only feel justified showing weakness when they're sick. I've also heard it said that men act like babies because they want their wives to coddle them like their mothers did. I'm not buying it. Mothers also showered love on their daughters when they were sick, but they didn't turn into Cruella de Vil.

Women are accustomed to pain and discomfort, starting with menstruation and on through labor and childbirth. When a woman feels sick, it rarely interferes with her lifestyle. She does laundry, washes dishes, takes a few minutes to throw up, carpools, and makes dinner. It's what she saw her mother and her grandmother do.

I think poet Maya Angelou must have had a man in mind when she wrote, "I've learned that even when I have pains, I don't have to be one."

NOT TO WORRY

BAD HABiTS

To break a bad habit, you must first accept that what you're doing is something you no longer want to do. Then, you must devise techniques that deter you from doing it again. Two facts must be present if you are to attain your goal: 1) You must really want this. 2) You must really want this.

I've had hundreds of bad habits over the years. Exaggeration, for one. Okay, maybe there were only three. One annoying habit I had was saying, "I'm sorry." I said it so often it made me, and everyone around me, nauseous. I apologized for everything I or anyone else said and did. Somewhere in my upbringing (yes, let's blame Mom and Dad), I was made to feel guilty about a great many things, whether or not they were my fault. "I'm sorry" somehow rectified all situations. The habit stuck. I'm still working on this, but I'm not quite over it. I'm sorry.

Another horrible habit was smoking. That was my mother's fault. She said I could smoke, but only at home, knowing full well that I would never do that. I suppose she assumed that if I wasn't smoking at home, I wasn't smoking. Dear Mother. She was sweet, trusting, and naive.

Over the years I quit about twenty-six times. Once I managed to cut down from one pack to one cigarette a day. I suspect I was kidding myself. I lit up, smoked, and put out that one cigarette repeatedly throughout the entire day. So while I technically had only one cigarette, I actually smoked over a dozen times.

I finally stopped, cold turkey. It was difficult, but doing it that way left no room for Should I or shouldn't I? decisions. Even after I hadn't had a cigarette for months, there were three crucial times I still longed for one: while talking on the phone, after dessert, and after sex. Taking a walk or potting a plant never suppressed the craving, so I relied on straws to replace the feeling of caressing a cigarette.

My friend Patti has tried to quit smoking for as long as I've known her. She makes it through two days, then buckles. Her last attempt was at an intervention when four friends and three family members endeavored to pull her off of a cigarette in the middle of a deep inhale. She fought like a hungry tiger. That inhale culminated into a colossal exhale that registered six on the Richter scale.

Dieting is a difficult habit to stick with. Obviously, I couldn't go cold turkey and stop eating, and I couldn't lick the same spoonful of cottage cheese all day long. Nor would I want to, but food is always on my mind. At breakfast I'm already thinking about dinner. It wouldn't be so bad if it weren't for my other bad habit: avoiding the gym. When my head was into it, two days in 2007, I showed up and worked out, but the bicycle and weight rooms were downstairs. I suggested to the owner that she put in an elevator.

"Wouldn't that defeat the purpose of going to the gym?" she asked.

I never got the connection, so I quit.

Just the thought of going was torture. Filled with conflict, I asked myself, Do I really feel like enduring torturous aches and pains and sweat today? I could always count on my answer being, "Is that a trick question?"

So my greatest bad habit is not really overeating. It's inactivity. The most exercise I get on any given day is sitting at my computer, typing. My fingers are capable of hammering out one hundred words per minute. I looked down at them recently and marveled at how lovely and slim they are.

I'm learning to type with my ass.

SiNFULLY MAHVELOUS

I was raised as a Conservative Jew, tilting heavily toward Orthodox. My father observed the laws of the Torah. My mother kept a kosher home, which included having separate sets of dishes and silverware for dairy and meat products. In addition, shellfish, pork, and certain cuts of beef were forbidden.

With this in mind, when I went off to college my greatest goal was not to obtain a BA or an MRS degree, like so many of my friends wanted. My goal was to taste bacon.

You should understand that I had always been a very good girl, doing exactly what was expected of me and never creating teenage waves of rebellion. Away from home for the first time, I wanted to feel the excitement of disobeying a rule. How better to do that than by eating bacon? I longed for it. The aroma had wafted through my nostrils many times at friends' homes, and I couldn't help but wonder how anything that smelled so wonderful could possibly be bad.

I had only been at college one day when I accepted a lunch date with a very handsome young man I'd met during registration. We went to a restaurant called The Carousel. The center of the restaurant, a huge, slowly rotating floor, was decorated like a merry-go-round.

I'd planned on casually ordering a bacon, lettuce, and tomato on white toast. Even the bread was a kind of rebellion.

Jews don't eat white bread. If it's not a heavy Russian or Jewish rye, it's not worth the calories.

Who would know? I was away from home. I was independent. I was with a very attractive stranger.

When the waitress came to our table, I acted like a worldly woman who had done this hundreds of times.

"I'd like a BLT on white toast, please." I'd always wanted to say that.

Sandy, my date, ordered tuna on rye.

When my food arrived I could barely contain myself. I bit into the sandwich. It was all I had hoped for. I wondered if I looked different. Could people tell I'd just crossed the line and taken my virgin bite of traif (non-kosher food)? I waited for a sign that what I'd done was okay—either that or a bolt of lightning.

As I pondered the enormity of the act, my date smiled and watched me eat.

"You're Jewish, aren't you?" he asked.

"Yes. Why?" Oh my God. I've been caught. Oh my God.

"No reason. I thought I saw a Star of David on a chain around your neck yesterday."

The combination of guilt and shame set in. I had swallowed a piece of loathsome, disgusting, filthy, cloven-hoofed, fried pig! The realization, plus the rotating floor, made me, in one swift motion, put down my sandwich, excuse myself, and cup my hand over my mouth. I bounded toward the edge of the spinning floor and prayed I wouldn't humiliate myself by throwing up. Then I remembered God, most likely, no longer viewed me as one of His chosen people so I didn't hold out much hope.

I thought about the chaos I'd cause if I got sick while standing on the edge of the rotating circular conveyor. Suddenly I found the strength to sprint to the ladies' room, where I threw up my guilt and thanked God for getting me there in time.

I returned to my date with renewed composure and fresh Sen-Sen breath. Our conversation eventually drifted toward the courses we were taking and what we wanted to do after college. I was to be a teacher or a secretary. My father had said they'd be good careers for me to fall back on when my husband died—like his death was an intrinsic part of the plan.

Sandy, to my utter mortification, wanted to follow in his father's footsteps and be a rabbi.

Kismet? Possibly. Coincidence? Maybe. But probably more like divine intervention because you'll never convince me that my father, looking down from heaven with great disappointment, didn't have a hand in this.

WHO SAYS BiGGER IS BETTER?

W hen Marc moved in with his worldly possessions, storage space in my home had already been assigned. Not only for my belongings, but for everything left to me by my deceased parents and brother. Closets overflowed. Shelves buckled from excessive weight. Halls and stairways were cluttered. Space under couches and beds no longer existed.

I didn't have a single drawer to offer him. They were all filled to capacity with treasured items, such as my high school club jacket and poodle skirts. I knew that one day I'd fit back into those twenty-one-inch waist cinchers and that beaver fur collars with furry ball ties would return to the fashion world. I'd be ready.

We decided to look for a larger house, one with trees and a pool, like we already had, but with more closets and no stairs. My arthritis made stair climbing increasingly difficult and we had to prepare for the future.

We found several lovely places, but when we figured out what expenses would be, we realized we could never afford to do anything except sit in the house and stare out the window.

We opted to expand.

After nearly two years of discussion, drawing architectural plans, and dealing with town bureaucracy, construction—or should I say destruction?—began on our home.

An army of men descended upon us, each in his own vehicle. Most of the first week was spent directing traffic with one goal—getting out of my driveway.

"If you move that forklift over here and the tractor over there, and José drives the bulldozer onto my neighbor's lawn, John can squeeze his pickup truck into that spot between those two boulders he just unearthed.

"Marc can drive his SUV onto the front porch so Javier can park his van over there, on our newly seeded lawn. Hopefully, that will leave enough room for me to back out onto the street and barely escape getting rear-ended by oncoming traffic."

We still haven't resolved the stair problem. We'll either put in an elevator or a stair lift. An elevator might work best in the speed department but it requires using a chunk of space from one of the rooms. Stair lifts are more space friendly, but unless they travel as fast as elevators, I could spend the better part of my remaining years staring at stairwell walls.

Although architectural drawings have been completed and sanctioned, and work has already begun, every day brings fresh ideas to my overactive, mercurial mind. Most include moving more walls, adding windows and, generally, ignoring permit-approved drawings.

Mighty Marc smiled through it all, and explained to the contractor, "My wife had another epiphany last night. This one includes moving the roof about two feet to the right. I hope that won't inconvenience you. Her job is to be creative. Mine is to keep her happy."

My husband's no dummy. To preserve his own sanity, he's learned how to appease me during critical times. He knows how cranky I get when I have to enter and exit my house through windows. He understands when I go berserk because a construction worker on a scaffold smiled at me through my second-floor bathroom window. He hugs my quaking body after I've endured eight hours of jackhammering. And he gently restrains me when I explain my need to hurt someone each time I pull carpenter nails out of my car tires.

I have no doubt the contractor is already looking forward to completing this project. His before and after pictures will not be of our home, but of the transformed woman living in the house. Her disrupted routine, nocturnal visions, and nonstop decisions will have changed her from perky and cheerful to jerky and tearful.

MARGIN FOR ERROR

There are three basic kinds of communication: verbal, in which you listen to comprehend; written, in which you read to understand; and nonverbal, in which you observe a person's actions or demeanor and draw a conclusion about their meaning.

Truth is, though, no matter how well you think you understand, the margin for error is huge.

In high school I took Shorthand and Speed Writing, both rapid, abbreviated forms of writing. I did this because, according to my father, learning to take dictation meant I could secure a secretarial position when—not if, but when—my husband died. I was seventeen, but he said this as though my future husband's death was a prerequisite for my secretarial career.

I was good at taking dictation but not so great at transcribing what I'd written, which was fine. It meant I didn't have to remain in any future marriage long enough for my husband to die. I never wanted to be a secretary—or a wife.

I wasn't a terrific student, so rather than struggle through several years of Spanish, I took it only long enough to learn how to order a margarita and find a bathroom in Mexico. Knowing more than that seemed superfluous.

Doctors have their own written language. It's only understood by other doctors, pharmacists, and some lab technicians. If you've ever tried to decipher a written prescription you, more than likely, experienced a pounding headache, profound eyestrain, and total bewilderment. I never had any interest in learning how to read doctors' prescriptions until last week, at LabCorp, when the phlebotomist preparing to draw my blood couldn't decipher whether my doctor's codes indicated he wanted my cholesterol or my PSA levels.

Hairdressers have their own language. It's taught in beautician school. It is in every woman's best interest to know Hairdresser before entering a salon. It isn't necessary to know the entire language. Just a select few words can make a difference in the quality of their lives.

For instance, every hairdresser knows what the word "trim" means, in Hairdresser language. But an innocent, unsuspecting woman who enters a salon with the intention of having just a teensy bit of hair snipped, does not realize her understanding of the word differs from that of her hairdresser. I learned this the hard way.

I sat in my hairdresser's chair.

"The length of my hair is pretty good," I said, "but I have an affair to attend tomorrow, so just clean it up a little." Then I used the words I assumed were universally understood. "Just a little trim."

My hairdresser confirmed her understanding of my request.

"Okay," she said. "Just a trim."

I felt no need to critique or analyze every snip-snip after that, although I admit I felt uneasy when she pulled out the electric razor and buzz cut around my ears. But she knew what I wanted, I reasoned, and I knew she knew what I wanted. So it wasn't an issue.

She scalped me.

I didn't have enough hair length to wrap around my curling iron. I'm convinced she is a descendant of an ancient Apache tribe.

Here's another communication lesson taught in beautician school: when a hairdresser screws up badly, her coworkers must jump in and lie their asses off.

I knew I was in trouble when every hairdresser in the shop stopped by and said, "Great cut," "You look fantastic," "I just love that style on you."

One hairdresser said, "It looks fantastic from the side."

"That might be a plus if I were Sidewinder," I answered. "Unfortunately, I usually enter a room facing front."

An example of visual misinterpretation occurred when I confessed to my friend, Rochelle, that every time I see an elderly couple walking arm in arm, I become teary eyed.

"It's beautiful to see they are still in love after so many years," I said.

Rochelle set me straight.

"Love has nothing to do with it," she said. "They're holding each other up."

I am now careful not to stand too close to my husband when we walk together. I want to make sure people recognize that we're in love. Not feeble.

Do IT YOURSELF

I t seems businesses have become smarter and we, the buying public, have become idiots. There was a time businesses bent over backwards to accommodate us, but now they have us doing their work for them—and then we pay them.

I live in the country where this practice seems to be most blatant. It may have started with Cut Your Own Christmas Tree Farms. People drive for miles from the suburbs into the country where they trudge through snow in hip boots, mufflers, mittens, and hats, in search of that one perfect tree. They struggle to chop it down, drag it to their vehicle, hoist it onto their car, and spend frustrating, bumbling moments securing it to their roofs so it won't take flight during their drive home. Their toes and noses are frozen, but they feel refreshed, invigorated, and happily pay the extra cost.

How about Pick Your Own Flowers? Situated on a garden center table are lovely fresh floral bouquets ready for purchase. But noooo, we'd rather walk into fields, through pollen, fighting off bees and myriad other insects in search of our own posies. Doing this makes us feel like Laura Ingalls Wilder.

Pick Your Own Strawberries, Blueberries, and Raspberries are popular summer activities at roadside stands. In the sweltering July heat, we see throngs of adults and children hunched over, like migrant workers, picking their way through fields of berries, examining and evaluating each one before gently dropping it into their pails.

Meanwhile, on a countertop of that same roadside stand, are those same berries, already packaged for lazy customers like me who would do anything to avoid bending and sweating.

We know fall is in the air when we see signs for places we can pick our own pumpkins. Pumpkins caked with mud and lying in fields are messy and heavy, but we enjoy surveying the huge selection, finding that perfect one, and lugging it to the cash register, rather than conveniently grabbing a clean one from the large display lined up on pallets. I suspect this is prompted by that same *Little House on the Prairie* syndrome.

I saw a sign at a roadside stand recently that read "Dig Your Own Mums" and, sure enough, people were lined up, shovels in hand, anxious to do just that. I don't know why they do it. I wouldn't. But apparently most people believe that muddy shoes and dirty hands are an integral part of communing with nature.

The one that makes me laugh out loud is Cook Your Own Food. It seems some high-end restaurants now invite customers to cook on their premises. They supply the food for the meal you choose to make.

I overheard several women discussing this phenomenon. Each expressed how wonderfully innovative the concept was. As far as I'm concerned, if I wanted to cook, I'd have stayed home and done it. Why would anyone in their right mind dress up, drive to a restaurant, and pay to cook their own dinner? I could do that in my own kitchen while wearing comfortable jeans and slippers.

Perhaps this is the start of a whole new American trend. I can see it now. The possibilities are endless: Cut Your Own Hair, Perform Your Own Colonoscopy, Dig Your Own Grave, and pay us for the privilege of letting you do it.

I received a bizarre e-mail recently. I don't usually open unsolicited mail, but this one captured my interest. I learned that anyone can send away for a diploma from most any college. They needn't attend classes or do anything even remotely cerebral to earn a degree. They need only to select the college of their choice, send in money, and wait for some faceless felon to mail them an "official" diploma. They can be the world's most pathetic, unmotivated, fifth-grade dropout, and still get a college degree to hang on the wall in their recently acquired suite of legal offices.

Ain't America great?

Do Not Disturb

Most nights I have a terrible time falling asleep. My mind is never fully at rest. I turn on my ceiling fan, winter and summer; punch my pillow to mold itself into my neck; pull up my quilt; get into position; and close my eyes. It's then I remember I have to phone Cynthia with directions to the restaurant we're meeting at Wednesday, work on a letter of recommendation for my granddaughter, and look for that pet insurance form that's buried somewhere on my desk. So right then and there, I reach for the sticky notes and pen on my end table and write reminder notes in the dark.

But my head continues to spin out of control with topic ideas for writing and decisions such as whether to drive into Manhattan, take the train, or get an Uber. It can be as long as forty-five minutes before I fall asleep, and then I can count on getting up for the bathroom at least three times. Consequently, most days I walk around in a zombie-like state.

Last night was a rare exception. Last night I was exhausted. I'd had a particularly physical day and it had knocked me out. I pulled the quilt over me at 11:45 p.m. and conked out immediately.

At 12:15 I was awakened with a loud ringing sound. I jumped up from a deep sleep, reached over, and smashed the button on my alarm clock. The ringing continued, so I reached for the phone. No one was on the line. I dragged myself out of bed and across the room in what felt like a drug-induced state.

Finally, I realized the ringing was coming from inside my purse. It was my cell phone.

Who the hell would call after midnight? Someone must have died or been in an accident. Oh no!

I grabbed the phone and saw the words: "FaceTime, Accept or Decline." As much as I use my cell phone for talking and messaging, I have never used FaceTime. Intentionally. I'm vain. If I were a younger version of myself, I wouldn't care one bit who saw what I look like waking up from a sound sleep, but I'm on the far, far, other side of fifty, and there's no way in hell I will ever allow myself to be seen without first spackling the crevices that cover my face and covering my head with a towel. My hair looked like I'd stuck my finger in a light socket.

But I was in a daze. I'd been awakened from a deep sleep. Without thinking, I pushed "Accept" and saw my granddaughter's face. She appeared to be at a party and having a good time … perhaps too good a time. She saw my face and yelled, "Hi, Grandma!"

Suddenly, I was wide awake and fully aware of what was happening. I sleep topless, and this girl had just seen her grandmother's face, neck, and naked chest, in a way she should never have had to. All I could think was, Poor baby. She's going to need therapy to erase that indelible picture from her mind.

Without uttering a sound, I disconnected.

As I stood there, wrapped in humiliation, I had another thought—a more pleasant one. Odds are that she never saw anything more than my wrinkled face, neck, and shoulders. My two main concerns were out of sight, resting on either side of my navel.

THiNGS THAT Go BUMP iN THE NiGHT

I t was 9 p.m. when I left the comfort of my bed and wandered into the kitchen to make a cup of herbal tea. When I turned on the light, the peripheral view of a gray blur bouncing up and down set off an involuntary shriek that shot up from my toes.

As my eyes focused I realized it was a mouse desperately trying to jump out of my sink. The terror that reduced my legs to water in no way interfered with the strength of my vocal cords, which were emitting ear-shattering obscenities I'd never heard flow from my lips before. After numerous valiant attempts, the three-inch beast succeeded in making it to my countertop.

We found ourselves staring at each other, neither of us moving. Instinctively, I believe we both knew I was expected to do something. But what? He certainly wasn't going to remain idle while I ran for a broom, and I was not about to do anything that could result in a messy countertop. Eventually, he tired of waiting and scurried off to wherever mice are instructed to go during their psychological warfare training.

Not knowing where he'd gone was worse than actually seeing him, so I flew down the hall to my bedroom, faster than I ever imagined my arthritic legs could move. Once there, I slammed the door shut and stuffed a huge afghan under it so he could not possibly get to me. This comforting feeling lasted about fifteen seconds until it occurred to me that Mickey had probably never entered a room through a doorway in his life. I sat in my bed, legs curled under me, not daring to let them hang over the edge. And there I remained for an undetermined amount of time.

I never saw or heard from Mickey again, but the thought that we were sharing my home was more than unsettling.

The next terrifying incident happened at my girlfriend's house in her newly decorated basement.

"What's that?" Carol screamed, pointing to a menacing black object on the floor. As I got closer I saw it was some kind of huge, horrifying insect. To stomp on it would ruin her new beige carpet, and because her fear was slightly more than mine, it became my responsibility to make it disappear.

"Hurry. Get me a cup to put over it before it gets away," I instructed.

Carol ran in confused, panicky circles and came back with an antique china cup.

"He's not staying for tea," I reminded her, so she left and returned with a paper cup.

As my heart pounded in my ears, I prepared to slam the cup over the revolting object of our terror and trap it. But as I lowered the cup over his disgusting black hairy body, I suddenly had a clear view of what had terrified us—a piece of knotted black yarn.

The next minutes were spent in convulsive laughter that found us competing to reach the bathroom.

IT'S ALL ABOUT ME

WHO AM I?

I wanted to gain insight into my ancestry, so I went online to 23andMe, filled out a form, and submitted it. In turn, they mailed me a kit that included a vial to spit into. My tongue, inner lips, and cheeks were raw from all the sucking required to withdraw enough saliva to reach the vial's half-inch marker.

I mailed the kit back and waited. I had visions of discovering an exciting past that included royalty, celebrities, or pioneers. Even a link to an infamous villain would have pleased me.

It didn't happen.

The DNA results arrived. After two hours of attempting to interpret countless pages of information, I learned I am 96.2 percent Ashkenazi Jewish. No surprise. And I have 1,290 DNA relatives. No surprise there either because I actually believe I know most of them already. On my father's side alone, there were eight children, each of whom had two or more children, who also had two or more children. We're considering holding our next family affair in Madison Square Garden.

I have 291 Neanderthal variants, which probably accounts for why I have trouble standing up straight. I've been blaming it on lower back arthritis, but I now suspect that it won't be long before my Neanderthal genes cause my knuckles to drag on the ground.

I also have minuscule amounts of other countries coursing through my veins, making me part Balkan, Southern European, and North African.

I phoned my Swedish girlfriend.

"Elsa," I said. "You'll be surprised to learn I have a little Scandinavian in me."

"Size doesn't matter," she said. "What's important is that he's kind to you."

There were three pages of diseases that I'm not likely to contract. Among them was one called Maple Syrup Urine Disease. After researching it I discovered it's a real disease and is quite serious. Given my love of pancakes, it seemed like something I should know about.

The results pointed out several other significant points of information. For instance, I'm not likely to sneeze after eating dark chocolate. I'll probably never know how accurate that finding is since I only like milk chocolate. I also learned I won't flush after drinking alcohol, which is another thing I'll probably never be able to prove since given the choice, I always choose milkshakes over alcohol.

One invaluable bit of information is the fact I move roughly sixteen times each hour that I'm asleep, which confirms and justifies the reason my husband relocated to another bed.

I'm also pleased to know I have only a 3 percent chance of developing a unibrow, and that my earlobes are detached from, as opposed to attached to, my face. That is exactly the kind of information I had been hoping to learn about myself.

While I admit that I enjoyed reading every bit of the DNA report, I feel the need to dispute several of the findings. In fact, I disagree to the point of laughing out loud.

My DNA suggests that my muscle composition is common in elite power athletes. In reality, if you Google "uncoordinated," my photo will appear. In grammar school my gym mates fought over me when selecting who they wanted on their softball or volleyball team.

"You take her," one team captain would shout.

"I don't want her. You take her," was the common response.

I was so clumsy, and without muscle power, that when it came time to climb the hanging ropes in the gym, I never got further than sitting on the knot.

My DNA indicates I am predisposed to weigh less than average. Less than the average what? Sumo wrestler? Blue whale? New Jersey ex-governor? Let's get this straight. I am NOT fat. What I am is curvy, a word once used to describe a stretch of road but lately is used to describe real women—women who never met a Twinkie they didn't like.

Quite possibly the most important bit of information I obtained from this test is the knowledge I am 75 percent more apt to smell asparagus metabolite in my own urine. That illuminating fact alone made the $200 I spent for this test worth every cent.

THANK YOU, ANDY ROONEY

Anyone who knows me will tell you my house is immaculate. I'm a neat freak. Even though I am a collector of many things, and my shelves, countertops, and walls are covered with photos and collectibles, nothing is disorganized. Everything has a place. Without order and serenity around me, I find it impossible to function.

Each morning I brew a cup of herbal tea and sip it as I roam from room to room patting myself on the back for the wonderful job I've done decorating each nook and cranny of my home. It suits me. It reflects who I am. The contemporary floral couch, off-white Berber carpeting, forest green ceiling rafters, original paintings, and wall hangings. It's who I am. Somehow I have managed to create a small piece of heaven for myself, and it brings me great pleasure.

Move farther down the hall—past my beckoning kitchen, past my inviting living room and cheerfully decorated bathroom. There is yet another door—on the right—that I keep closed at all times.

You know how in horror movies there's always that one room that the overnight guest has been warned not to enter? And the guest, sensing something terrible is beyond that door, is helplessly drawn to opening it, anyway?

That's the door to my office, otherwise known as my Inner Sanctum.

Before entering I place one hand on the doorknob and slowly nudge the door open, inch by inch. I do not attempt to enter the room all at once. To do so would send me into a tailspin. As I peer through the widening crack, I place one foot into the room with the caution of a soldier in a minefield. I expect to see Rod Serling standing there, waiting to welcome me into The Twilight Zone.

I grab hold of the shovel leaning against the wall and plow my way toward the desk that I can't actually see though I do recall it being on the left side of the room.

At first glance you might think you're in the office of a deranged hoarder. Within seconds, you are convinced of it.

My beautiful off-white carpeting is not visible. It is blanketed with books, papers, magazines, and file folders I will find a proper home for tomorrow, tomorrow, and tomorrow. And my desktop? What desktop? It's five inches deep with papers of all sizes and colors, newspaper clippings, financial statements, countless sticky notes, more books, and articles—all of which I'm going to file, pay, or read either later today or, certainly, one day this year.

It's not my fault. I leave neatly stacked paperwork on my desk before retiring each evening, but those frisky little papers must fool around all night because by morning they've reproduced. At least I'm pretty certain that's what happens.

This morning I entered my office with the intention of making a dent in the mess. I shuffled through some of the debris and was thrilled to discoverer I have a lovely cranberry-colored, leather, in/out box that I seem to recall matches a wastebasket I know is buried somewhere under the desk. It appears this room was once nicely decorated.

Awhile back I spoke with a shrink about this discrepancy in my personality.

"Why, oh why," I whined, "am I not able to keep my office neat? I try so hard. I should think that being well organized would be a priority for me as a writer, if my creative juices are to flow."

He disagreed and said the disorderly part of my personality actually reflects my creativity. I mulled that over for a few minutes, after which I handed him $90, walked out, and decided he was the one in need of counseling.

Some time ago the late Andy Rooney took us viewers into the offices of each member of the 60 Minutes staff. To my utter shock I saw that Lesley Stahl, Morley Safer, and Andy himself all had offices that very much resembled mine. One office actually looked worse than mine. Its couch was entirely buried in books and file folders. There was no place on it to sit.

Perhaps my shrink was onto something. But what I'd like to know is, are creative people genetically disorganized, are disorganized people inherently creative, and would I have more storage room if I bought a couch?

TELL ME SOMETHING I ALREADY KNOW

I went to a psychic fair with my daughter. We weren't in search of anything but fun. I paid for a twenty-minute session with a psychic, anticipating nothing more than twenty minutes of skepticism and amusement.

I sat across the table from her. She cocked her head, furrowed her brows, and said, "You look so familiar. Don't I know you?"

I couldn't resist.

"Shouldn't you know that? I think I deserve a refund."

We laughed as I prepared to be entertained by a fraudster.

"Your mother has tried to communicate with you," she said.

"How?"

"By way of her perfume, White Shoulders, I believe."

Whoa! My mother had worn White Shoulders.

I didn't say a word.

She then asked if I'd recently been aware of that scent.

"No," I answered, "and what does that even mean?"

Before she had a chance to respond, I recalled an incident that had happened several weeks earlier. I had come downstairs to our garage, where my husband was waiting in the car. I opened the car door.

"Who was just here?" I asked.

"No one," he answered. "Why?"

"There's a strong scent of perfume. It's lovely and smells strangely familiar. Someone was here. Don't you smell it?"

"No. I don't smell anything."

"How can you not smell it?" I asked, incredulously. "It's so strong."

I said no more about it and accepted that my sense of smell was sharper than his.

The fragrance lingered in both the car and our house for several days. Although I continued to be baffled, I eventually forgot about it.

Until I sat before the psychic, who then told me my father had died in his mid-forties, my mother was strikingly beautiful and enjoyed dressing up, and my brother had died a tragic death shortly before he turned fifty.

She was correct on every count. My father had died at forty-six, my mother was stunning, and my brother had been killed in a motorcycle accident three weeks before his fiftieth birthday and the enormous party I'd been planning for him.

I left the psychic with a wonderful feeling of well-being. I felt my mother's strong presence.

My daughter and I enjoyed falafel and hummus from the fair's food trucks, then walked across the street to a building with a large room where three psychics were on stage. They were taking turns at trying to match the spirit visions in their heads to specific people in the audience.

Psychic: "A woman is talking to me. She is from Ireland. She is telling me that she made oatmeal for her son every day when he was growing up. This woman has red hair."

A man in the audience began flailing his arms and shouting.

"That's me! I'm the son. I'm from Ireland. My mother had red hair, and she made me porridge every day. In fact, I still eat it. Every day."

Psychic: "And I see a woman whose name starts with 'T.' She's a younger woman. Do you know who she is?"

"Yes. Theresa. Theresa was my sister. Oh my God. Oh my God."

The psychic touched two fingers to her forehead and closed her eyes.

"Is there someone in your family whose name begins with 'B'?"

"Yes. Yes. My son, Brian. Holy %@#$! This is amazing."

"Your mother asks that you please take care of your diabetes."

"Huh? What diabetes? I don't have diabetes."

"Are you certain?"

While he pondered the possibility of having diabetes, another hand shot up from the other side of the room.

"Me! Me! I have diabetes. I have diabetes. I'm from Ireland, and I eat oatmeal."

"Do you have someone in your family whose name begins with 'B'?"

"Does it have to be a person? My dog's name is Bingo. Does that count?"

"And what about the person whose name starts with 'T'?"

"My ex-wife, Toni. Does it matter that we've been divorced for nine years? We have a nice relationship."

"And your mother. Did she have red hair?"

"Sometimes."

The psychic turned back to the first Irishman, who was feverishly chewing his nails.

"I'm so sorry," she said to him. "It appears that Irishman number two, with diabetes, is the correct Irishman."

"But that's crazy. Dogs shouldn't count," he protested. "And my doctor said if I don't lose weight, I could become pre-diabetic. That should count for something. Right?"

My daughter and I slipped out of the room with our hands cupped over our mouths, trying hard not to choke on our laughter.

I'm not sure why I go to these things, but I suspect it's because of my age and my desperate need to believe everything doesn't end just because we die.

WHEN THE LiFE YOU PLANNED BACKFiRES

'm on the computer every day. I'm there to do research and to write. While I sit at my desk, people send me videos of puppies and babies doing adorable things. Since I was born without the ability to ignore distractions, I'm always compelled to stop what I'm doing and watch. This accounts for why I never get anything done.

The videos that particularly hold me in abeyance are those that showcase limber, graceful, athletic octogenarians performing activities that people half their age might find daunting. They jitterbug at a brisk tempo with supreme agility. They run marathons and perform flawlessly on parallel bars. They scale mountains like sure-footed mountain goats and roller blade like fearless teenagers.

These videos inspire, encourage, and motivate. They point out what I have heard so often: age is merely a state of mind.

But, mostly, they piss me off.

My plan for aging was different from the one I'm living. I had hoped to be a shining example of what later years can and should be. I was going to parachute jump, throw rowdy parties, and dance with abandon. I planned to be quirky and free-spirited. I would wear flashy costume jewelry, spike heels, travel the world alone, and dance barefoot in foreign courtyards. I looked forward to shrugging off rules and being unconventional whenever possible. My goal was to galvanize senior couch potatoes into action.

I was well on my way to living my dream when the universe yanked my arm and shouted, "Whoa! Slow down, lady. That ain't gonna happen. Time to focus on Plan B."

Plan B? What Plan B? I didn't have a Plan B.

It wasn't long before Plan B showed up and took over. All I could do was watch. It was nothing like my original plan. Fun was replaced with various levels of pain, including but not limited to debilitating arthritis, atrial fibrillation, and constant shoulder and neck discomfort.

I crossed zip lining off my list.

Plan B required a whole different mind-set. There would be no traveling by myself, no roller blading, bungee jumping, or fast dancing. The most physical thing I would do is press the start button on my Jazzy scooter. I could still throw parties and wear party hats, but I would be more of a spectator than a participant.

It was during this self-pitying period that a different type of video captured my attention: videos of severely disabled men and women triumphing over their disabilities, accomplishing tasks far beyond anyone's expectations. Some of them were missing limbs. One young woman was born without the entire lower half of her body. One man was without his upper left side—shoulder, arm, and torso.

To watch the spirit and determination of these incredible human beings brought me to my knees. These superheroes had ignored naysayers, and with blind conviction and belief in themselves, forged ahead and made their impossible dreams come true.

I was embarrassed. It hadn't occurred to me to attempt some of the activities I assumed I could no longer do. I had accepted my limitations as the final word.

How dare I whine because this latter part of my life didn't turn out as I'd planned? Wasn't it enough that I was still here? Many people my age no longer were. Yes, I am always with a degree of pain, but wasn't it fantastic that I had no debilitating illness that confined me to bed? And even if I couldn't do all I wanted, it wasn't as though there weren't activities I could still enjoy, such as traveling with my loving husband. I wouldn't be jitterbugging, but I could snap my fingers to the beat, sing out loud, and sway in my chair.

So, yes, age is a state of mind. And by mind, I mean attitude. The right attitude can be the difference between peace of mind and discontentment.

My father was a God-fearing man. When I was a child I'd ask him, "Can we go to the movies Saturday?" or "Can Nancy sleep over Friday?" His response to any question involving the future was always the same: "If we live and we're well."

I never knew why he was so seemingly negative. Years later his words made sense when I came upon a Yiddish proverb, "Man plans and God laughs." My father understood that the outcome of any plan is not entirely up to us.

FOLLOWING MY BLISS

A while back, I caught an old taped television show of Bill Moyers interviewing Joseph Campbell about his book, *The Power of Myth*. I suddenly realized Campbell was talking about me.

It appears that what I've been doing most of my life is struggling to "follow my bliss." According to Campbell, this means always listening closely to the voice within you. The voice may lead you to sacrifice. It may lead you to challenge. It could even lead you away from fortune, but it will direct you to the greatest and purest joys of fulfillment—your own true needs. Not desires, but needs.

Campbell asserts that we all have a little voice within that guides us toward what we instinctively know will make us happy. But most of us don't hear it or ignore it because we are moving too fast, anxious to get on with the next project that will take us to what we believe will fulfill us—fame, fortune, sexual gratification.

But, he says, if we take the time to stop and listen, really listen, we will know exactly what we need to be happy.

Over the years I have been fortunate to hear that voice, but during the first part of my life, I ignored it. My confidence was low, and I didn't believe that my needs, thoughts, or ideas were valid or mattered.

In the middle of my life I acknowledged my right to reach for my bliss, but there were those who stood in my way and discouraged me from reaching because my bliss conflicted and interfered with their plans for me. And that is why, in this last part of my life, I struggle with every fiber of my body to be true to myself.

It often has been difficult to remain focused on life's long, bumpy path. It has meant forgoing some pleasures, losing some friendships, and sometimes being viewed as bewildering. The fallout often saddens me. But when I deviate from my path toward bliss to appease the desires—not needs—of others, I find they feel grateful and I feel diminished and further from my goal.

Following one's bliss does not equate with hedonism, self-gratification, or self-indulgence. Not at all. It simply means you should always know what you need in this world to bring you the most fulfillment.

I do not strive to be unreasonable or antisocial but only to have peace of mind, a peace that eludes me unless I'm totally true to myself and in touch with my needs.

I've reached an age when I fully believe that I've earned the right to follow my bliss and that I should be able to do so without fear of controversy or conflict.

DANCiNG THROUGH THE PAiN

I opened an e-mail that promised a video of a ninety-four-year-old woman dancing the two-step. She entered the dance floor just as one might expect from a woman her age: she moved slowly, haltingly, and pushed a walker.

Her dance partner, a much younger man, attempted to take her walker from her. She resisted. But at the end of the charade, she pushed the walker away, and the two of them danced. Her moves were fluid, her body limber. And, if you know what a two-step is, you know it requires more than agility and strength. It calls for a sharp mind.

I want to be that woman when I'm ninety-four. I'd like to be that woman now! I love to dance, and if I do say so, I used to be pretty darn good at it. I even won a couple of jitterbug contests back in the mid-1950s.

Then I married a man who had no interest in dancing, so I spent twenty-three years at weddings and bar mitzvahs doing nothing more than tapping my feet.

In the next chapter of my life I married Mighty Marc, the best dancer I've ever known. In fact, he used to teach the instructors at Arthur Murray Dance Studios. But, as fate would have it, after finally landing a man who dances, my arthritis doesn't allow me to do more than stand in his arms and sway to the music.

I'm not particularly happy with all the negative changes my aging body has been forced to accept. My body has been undergoing changes from the day I was born, but most, such as growing breasts, brought positive results. Now the only things growing are my nose, ears, and hips.

Recently I had a mammogram. The technician looked at me and said, "You have beautiful, well-defined shoulders." I'd never had someone compliment my shoulders before so I didn't know how to react. I decided to tell the truth.

"Thank you," I said, "but those protruding, well-defined shoulder bones are actually the result of arthritis."

My hairdresser had the audacity to point out what she described as "a few gray hairs." I quickly kicked that thought to the curb.

"You're wrong!" I growled. "I do not have gray hairs. Look again."

She reexamined the strands.

"You're right," she recanted. "I don't know how I could have made such a mistake. They're blonde."

Aging doesn't just manifest as wrinkles and gray hair. It shows in more subtle ways, too. For instance, Mighty Marc and I have been together for more than fifteen years and the three little words he used to say to me so often have changed to, "I gotta pee." On our last road trip, we selected the longer route to our destination because the shorter one didn't provide rest stops every ten miles.

Once I was in the bedroom, rushing to get dressed and out of the house, when Mighty Marc walked in and found me standing in nothing more than a pair of black panties.

"Are you ready yet?" he asked.

My brows furrowed.

"Do I look ready?"

After checking me out for a few seconds, he said, "You could use some lipstick."

There was a time when walking into the bedroom and finding me in a state of undress would have brought about an entirely different response. Back then he wouldn't have noticed, or cared, if I was headless.

I once greeted my first husband at the door naked and wrapped in Saran. Being his usual pragmatic self, he looked at me and asked, "Aren't you cold? Where are the kids? What's for dinner?"

What a terrible waste of plastic wrap.

CONFLiCTED

A
t the end of long, tiring days, when I'm talked out, bleary eyed, and in need of total distraction, I go to Facebook. It's there I laugh at jokes, savor aphorisms, read skewed political opinions, and learn valuable life lessons, such as "The Correct Way to Fold Socks," which takes three times longer than rolling them into a ball the way I do because personally, I don't care if my socks are wrinkled. I also learned "How to Boil and Peel an Egg." (Shame on me. I've been doing it wrong my entire life.)

On Facebook I've been asked to pray for gravely ill strangers to recover, individuals to pass tests, lame dogs to walk, and a turtle who wouldn't eat. One distraught dimwit put out a call for prayers when her nail had the audacity to break on a Sunday, and she couldn't find a nail technician to repair it.

I thought of the legions of needy Facebook strangers counting on my prayers and opted not to waste one on her. She already had twenty-three Likes, and one Heart, so I figured she was covered.

I've received countless friend requests from men in uniform, too, all claiming to be American born. Each has the American flag on his cover page but barely speaks English. One man wrote that he's "looking for to love a woman. I have a son and my wife is late since two years ago." If for no other reason, this man has to be admired for his incredible patience.

Facebook's messaging is the best thing to happen to me since I had my eyebrows tattooed. It allows me to stay in touch with people I care about and meet new people I otherwise wouldn't. And I can do it all on my own time schedule, at my own convenience. It's the solution to a lifetime of internal conflict concerning how to keep friends without having to actually talk to them.

It's not that I don't like my friends. I care deeply for them. But am I morally bound to answer the phone if I'm involved in a project, or in the middle of creating the Great American Novel, even though that interruption would cause my thoughts to splinter into a million pieces I'd never be able to recreate?

My phone is trained to take messages. Am I a horrible person if I listen to someone leave a message, then make a mental note to return their call when it's more convenient, like sometime before I die?

And when the doorbell rings, is it okay if I drop to the floor and freeze until I'm sure they've left, the way I usually do? Or must I stop what I'm doing, paste on a happy face, and be polite to the two well-dressed Bible-carrying men who aren't in the slightest bit interested in the fact that I'm not in the slightest bit interested? And do I have to open the door to cute little Girl Scouts selling cookies I don't want? If I buy them, I eat them and get fat. Past attempts at hiding them from myself have been unsuccessful.

Mind you, I might be able to handle a phone interruption if it lasted five minutes, but an average phone call between female friends can last forty-five minutes to an hour.

Men don't have this problem. They use the phone the way God intended—with a specific purpose in mind.

"Hi, Bob. Are you up for a round of golf Sunday?" — "Great. I'll text you with the specifics."

My idea of the perfect phone call length.

Mighty Marc received a call from his friend Barry. When he hung up he looked at me and said, "Diane died."

I gasped.

"What?! When? What happened?"

"All I know is she's dead."

"But she was only eighty-five. Had she been ill? Did she suffer? Was she alone? When's the funeral? I'll have to buy a black dress."

"He didn't say anything else."

"Why didn't you push for more details? Details are important."

"No. They're not. All you need to know is she's dead."

I, of course, had to phone several friends to report Diane's passing, at the cost of one hour per conversation.

So, if you're interested in not spending endless time on the phone, go to Facebook. It enlightens, educates, creates, and promotes friendships, precipitates laughter, provides purpose to otherwise lonely lives, and, best of all, allows you to enjoy brief, written conversations at your leisure and convenience without ever having to say a word.

WAiTING To SERVE OUR COUNTRY

Here we sit. In the Jury Room Holding Tank. Waiting to fulfill our moral and legal obligation. Waiting to be called into the courtroom. Anxious to aid in combatting crime. Happy there are vending machines.

The courthouse parking lot is full. We parked on the street and run out to feed our meters every hour—a welcome break, actually, but for below-freezing temperatures.

It's been three hours since we arrived. Promptly. As directed. We canceled appointments, hired babysitters, skipped work, swapped car pool dates, missed bridge games, and rescheduled vacations.

We come in all sizes, shapes, and colors, from every walk of life. We sit, stand, slouch, slump, and wiggle in incredibly uncomfortable hard metal chairs. We are friendly, sociable, timid, distant, gregarious, apprehensive, outgoing, and cranky. Mostly, we are bored.

We read books, peruse newspapers, read candy wrappers, shuffle through magazines, tear out articles, rip out recipes, chew gum, blow bubbles, do crossword puzzles, play Sudoku, and make shopping lists.

We discuss our children, our parents, our spouses, our ex-spouses, and our amazing grandchildren. We express our opinions about Iran, Iraq, Israel, Syria, China, immigration, Social Security, Obama, Trump, the Kardashians, Roe v. Wade,

George Clooney, equal rights, birth control, transgender restrooms, long-term health care, prescription costs, gas prices, declining morality, and the increasing use of profanity.

We use our cell phones to call friends, call home, call our stockbrokers, call our babysitters, call our bookies, tweet, check Facebook, and play solitaire and Candy Crush.

We consume pretzels, sandwiches, potato chips, rice cakes, candy bars, cookies, coffee, soda, and yogurt.

We stare at the ceiling, stare into space, examine our palms, play with our buttons, pick at our cuticles, cough, yawn, sneeze, and nap, somehow managing to not fall off our chairs.

We walk to the back of the room and back to the front of the room, sit down, shift from one cheek to the other cheek, stretch, and stare glassy-eyed out the window at citizens freely walking, driving, laughing, shopping, and enjoying life when they should be here with us, questioning the accuracy of their watches and dying of tedium while waiting to proudly serve our country.

God bless America.

MORE ABOUT LAVERNE

Throughout my school years, I panicked whenever I had to write an essay. What would I say? Why would anyone be interested? Many years later, I accepted an invitation to take over the Parent/Teacher newsletter at my children's grammar school. It was then that I fell in love with words and their power to stimulate, motivate, and influence. It was the first step to a fulfilling life of writing.

I collaborated in writing a humorous play that successfully eradicated existing discord between parents and faculty. I went on to work with the school system's psychologist to create a series of Behavior Modification skits to benefit parents and teachers.

Throughout the 1970s, I wrote human interest stories and press releases for the *West Essex Tribune* and the *Star-Ledger* newspapers. I then joined the writing staff of sister publications, *Northern Horizon* and *Montague* magazines. My assignments included provocative topics such as How to turn doilies into Valentines, How to decorate tissue boxes with gold sprayed macaroni, and What to do if confronted by a bear, in the woods. For those who are interested, the answer is scream, and bang pots and pans, which only work if you remember to bring them with you on your hike.

In 1999 my column, "Laverne's View," was published in *Fifty Plus Monthly*, a regional New Jersey newspaper with a large readership. The column caught on and nearly every day brought emails and letters from appreciative readers.

Senior Wire News Service picked up my column for syndication in 2004 and is read nationally.

In 2012 my first book, *How the (Bleep) Did I Get This Old?* was published. Within hours of its release I was flooded with emails from publications across the country and Australia asking me to blog for them. *Forbes* and *Huff Post* were among those that reached out to me. I accepted Huff Post.

The onslaught of non-stop emails and phone calls continued for several exhausting, exciting months.

My writing has appeared in, to name a few, *Huff Post*, *Reader's Digest*, *Mature Living*, *Woman's Hockey*, *Big Apple Parent*, TrueHumor.com, *After Fifty Living*, and the *Daily Record* newspaper. Some anthologies that include my writing are *Story House*, *Rocking Chair Reader*, *Bedpan Banter*, *Craft of the Modern Writer*, and *Columnists: While We're Still Around*.

I was interviewed by international radio host Carol Marks on her show *A Touch of Grey*. Brian Feinblum interviewed me for his book marketing buzz blog, and Bottom Line Retirement interviewed me twice, for its national publication.

Driving Backwards on a One-Way Street: A Sassy Senior's Map to Finding Humor in Everything is my second collection of laugh-out-loud syndicated columns.

I live with my artistic husband, Marc Cicchetto, and our pampered Bichon Frise, Shadeaux, who was born in France and barks like an air horn, but with a French accent. Marc and I met online in 2003. We live in Newton, New Jersey where we enjoy all the perks of country living.

Being a breast cancer survivor has contributed significantly to my immense love for, and appreciation of, life.

Made in the USA
Middletown, DE
07 October 2020